Cambridge Elements

Elements in Development Economics
Series Editor-in-Chief
Kunal Sen
UNU-WIDER and University of Manchester

GENDER ECONOMICS IN THE GLOBAL SOUTH

Olivia Bertelli
University Paris-Dauphine, PSL

Shaftesbury Road, Cambridge CB2 8EA, United Kingdom

One Liberty Plaza, 20th Floor, New York, NY 10006, USA

477 Williamstown Road, Port Melbourne, VIC 3207, Australia

314–321, 3rd Floor, Plot 3, Splendor Forum, Jasola District Centre, New Delhi – 110025, India

Cambridge University Press is part of Cambridge University Press & Assessment, a department of the University of Cambridge.

We share the University's mission to contribute to society through the pursuit of education, learning and research at the highest international levels of excellence.

www.cambridge.org
Information on this title: www.cambridge.org/9781009576352

DOI: 10.1017/9781009576369

© UNU-WIDER 2026

This publication is in copyright. Subject to statutory exception and to the provisions of relevant collective licensing agreements, with the exception of the Creative Commons version the link for which is provided below, no reproduction of any part may take place without the written permission of Cambridge University Press & Assessment.

An online version of this work is published at doi.org/10.1017/9781009576369 under a Creative Commons Open Access license CC-BY-NC-SA 3.0 IGO which permits re-use, distribution and reproduction in any medium for non-commercial purposes providing appropriate credit to the original work is given, any changes made are indicated, and the new work is published under the same licence terms. When the licensor is an intergovernmental organisation, disputes will be resolved by mediation and arbitration where possible. To view a copy of this license, visit https://creativecommons.org/licenses/by-nc-sa/3.0/igo

When citing this work, please include a reference to the DOI 10.1017/9781009576369

First published 2026

A catalogue record for this publication is available from the British Library

A Cataloging-in-Publication data record for this Element is available from the Library of Congress

ISBN 978-1-009-57635-2 Hardback
ISBN 978-1-009-57637-6 Paperback
ISSN 2755-1601 (online)
ISSN 2755-1598 (print)

Additional resources for this publication at www.cambridge.org/bertelli

Cambridge University Press & Assessment has no responsibility for the persistence or accuracy of URLs for external or third-party internet websites referred to in this publication and does not guarantee that any content on such websites is, or will remain, accurate or appropriate.

For EU product safety concerns, contact us at Calle de José Abascal, 56, 1°, 28003 Madrid, Spain, or email eugpsr@cambridge.org

Gender Economics in the Global South

Elements in Development Economics

DOI: 10.1017/9781009576369
First published online: March 2026

Olivia Bertelli
University Paris-Dauphine, PSL

Author for correspondence: Olivia Bertelli, olivia.bertelli@dauphine.psl.eu

Abstract: Despite past progress toward gender equality, recent trends reveal a stagnating – or even reversing – situation since 2019. According to recent estimates, full parity is to be reached in 134 years, shifting this achievement from 2030 to 2158. Women still exhibit worse conditions than men everywhere in the world, but the gender gaps are particularly stark in the global South. This Element provides an overview of cutting-edge research in the economics of gender inequality in the global South, while offering a snapshot of women's living conditions using recent worldwide available data. The evidence reviewed encompasses a large set of possible solutions to end gender inequality, from policy reforms that ban discriminatory practices and grant equal rights to men and women, to antipoverty programs, as well as interventions facilitating women's access to formal education and the labor market. This title is also available as open access on Cambridge Core.

Keywords: gender inequality, global South, discrimination, son preference, child marriage, gender-based violence

© UNU-WIDER 2026

ISBNs: 9781009576352 (HB), 9781009576376 (PB), 9781009576369 (OC)
ISSNs: 2755-1601 (online), 2755-1598 (print)

Contents

	Preface	1
1	Introduction	2
2	Development and Gender Inequality: A Bidirectional Relationship	6
3	Son Preference	21
4	Child Marriage: Determinants and Policy Responses	25
5	Gender-Based Violence	38
6	The Overarching Role of Gendered Cultural Traits and Social Norms	50
7	Conclusive Remarks, Paths for Future Research, and a Policy Road Map	67
	References	73

An online appendix for this publication can be accessed at www.cambridge.org/bertelli

Preface

Women's conditions have massively improved in the past 100 years. The structural transformation most countries have gone through has considerably changed women's lives from one generation to the other. Simply looking at how my grandmother's life differed from mine, or that of my mother, gives me a sense of this dramatic change.

Born after World War I, my grandmother grew up in an Italian wealthy family and was given access to secondary education. Fairly young, she married a man of an aristocratic and wealthy family, but after he was captured during World War II she managed to annul the marriage and married my grandfather. She had again married a wealthy man, but this time her husband was a politically active journalist of liberal and republican ideas. Yet he was an awful man at home. She gave birth to three daughters, one after the other with little birth spacing and no birth control. She never engaged in any economic activity and remained financially dependent on her husband. Her position at home differed greatly from her status as a citizen of the newborn Italian Republic, which granted civil and political rights to women before family rights. Allowed to vote in elections from 1945, women remained subject to a patriarchal family code for much longer. In 1966 the trial of Franca Viola marked a turning point, as she was the first woman in Italy to refuse to marry her raper at a time when, absent any legislation against gender-based violence, the law instead absolved a raper if he agreed to marry his victim. This legislation, in force till 1981, echoed a popular custom that expected young (minor) women to marry their raper.

My grandmother's life strongly differed from that of my mother, who was free to choose her university field of study, her work activity, whether to marry and with whom, and whether and when to have children. This is not to say that all women of my mother's generation encountered the same freedom as she did. Italy still today scores the largest labor force participation gender gap in the European Union – 19.4 percentage points against an average of 10 – and gender-biased attitudes persist.[1]

The legal reforms and societal changes Western countries – and several others – encountered during the twentieth century have much improved women's conditions and agency, setting them legally free to choose and set their own lives. Rights, such as political rights, divorce, contraceptives, autonomously owning a bank account, and signing a work contract, are fairly

---

[1] https://ec.europa.eu/eurostat/statistics-explained/index.php?title=Gender_statistics#Labour_market. Thirty percent of the Italian population holds a biased view about women's economic role in the society and 54% believe that being a housewife is as fulfilling as working for pay and that when a mother works for pay, her children suffer (World Values Survey 2017–2022).

recent achievements that date back to less than a century ago. Despite these dramatic improvements, worldwide most countries still legally discriminate against women, while biased social norms and attitudes against women remain common. Benefiting from a wealthy living condition did not make my grandmother's survival any easier in a stringent patriarchal society. Italy's rapid economic growth did not help her escape violence. Apart from her own resilience, it was the legal reforms and societal changes (especially the students' and women's civic movements) that came along with economic development that allowed her to achieve her own freedom.

This Element questions the view that the structural transformation brought by economic development will be sufficient to eradicate gender inequality. Targeted policies granting equal rights and facilitating women's access to the labor market, along with a radical drift toward more progressive attitudes, behaviors, and social norms, are a pressing need to be addressed worldwide.

1 Introduction

Gender equality is still far from achieved. The world is not on track to achieve the United Nations' (UN) Sustainable Development Goal (SDG) number 5 aimed at reaching gender equality and empowering all women and girls, nor is it on track to achieve all the other gender-related indicators and targets of the UN's 2030 Agenda. Despite a remarkable increase in the human development of the world population, be it in terms of life expectancy at birth, of years of schooling, or of gross national income per capita, women's living conditions still lag behind those of men. As of today, the latest figures from the Human Development Index show that men exhibit higher human development than women across all world regions, in poor countries as well as in rich countries. Despite an increase in gender equality since 1990, recent trends show a stagnating – or even reversing – situation since 2019. At the current rate of progress, it will take 134 years to reach full parity, shifting the achievement of SDG 5 to 2158 (WEF, 2024). The loss in progress is remarkable knowing that in 2020 the global gender gap was expected to be closed within 100 years (WEF, 2022).

While the factors contributing to this stagnating situation are yet to be formally established and quantified, the global Covid-19 pandemic likely played a pivotal role, both at the individual and at the country level. At the individual level, containment measures and lockdowns increased women's domestic unpaid care workload and exposure to domestic violence. Across high- and middle-income countries job losses, especially for low-educated women with young children and unable to work from home, have been significantly worse for women than for men, unlike other past recessions that have historically affected male workers more than female workers (Goldin, 2022; Berniell, et al. 2023). In low-income countries women transitioned from wage employment to self-employment, mostly in agriculture and other unskilled sectors misaligned with their skill sets, widening the gender pay gap (Alfonsi, Namubiru, & Spaziani, 2024). At the country level, the economic impact of Covid strained countries' economic resources, disrupting public services, such as educational, training and childcare programs, that usually facilitate women's participation in the labor market (WEF, 2022). Following the disruption of public programs, such as family planning, access to contraceptives, and prevention of child marriage and female genital mutilation, it is estimated that 1.4 million unintended pregnancies, 10 million additional child marriages, and 2 million more female genital mutilations that would have otherwise been avoided are expected to occur by 2030 (WEF, 2024).

These budget cuts have been echoed by a decrease in bilateral Official Development Aid (ODA) with gender equality objectives. The ODA share devoted to gender equality projects and programs dropped from 45% to 42% between 2019 – 2020 and 2021 – 2022, and disbursements have stagnated since 2020 (OECD, 2024). Of the 32 OECD Development and Assistance Committee members (DAC), 20 focused less on gender equality in 2021 – 2022 than in 2019 – 2020. The slight upturn in 2023 did not restore the 2019 levels. In 2022 – 2023, no country had reached the international target of funding at least 85% of projects with a principal or significant gender equality objective, and only the Netherlands and Spain had devoted at least 20% of their ODA to the direct promotion of equality.[2] Out of the $68.7 billion per year committed by the OECD-DAC donors toward gender equality, only 8.3% (equivalent to 3.8% of total bilateral ODA) is directed to projects reporting gender equality as the principal objective. The UN Trade and Development organization estimates a yearly funding gap of $420 billion to achieve gender equality by 2030 in all developing countries.[3]

Apart from recent crises and gaps in funding from the international community, the root causes of gender inequality are historical, complex, and interrelated. Persistent discrimination in social institutions – the established set of formal and/or informal laws, norms, and practices present in a society – certainly contribute to the lasting inequalities and inequities that women face. Still today, almost 40% of the countries in the world report a medium/high/very high level of gender discrimination in social institutions (OECD, 2023).

---

[2] https://focus2030.org/which-countries-support-gender-equality-in-their-official-development.
[3] https://unctad.org/sdg-costing/gender-equality.

Gender-unequal laws and social norms fundamentally dictate women's and men's roles in the society, creating and reinforcing inequalities between men and women. For women these include unequal access to work, asset ownership, and inheritance, limited civil and political rights, and higher vulnerability to violence. By restricting women's and girls' autonomy, discriminatory social institutions have far-reaching effects on various aspects of their lives, from sexual and reproductive health rights to exposure to violence, economic opportunities, political representation, and decision-making power in both the private and public spheres. For the most part these laws, norms, and practices are deep-rooted in societies and evolve little over time. Understanding their origins and how they can be turned more egalitarian represents the object of a prosperous academic literature in economics during the past 10 years or so.

As a matter of fact, analyzing the causes and exploring possible solutions to gender inequality constitutes the essence of a blooming research field in economics – as well as in social sciences and humanities – across the global North and the global South. This Element aims at providing an overview of a selection of cutting-edge research in development economics on gender inequality while offering a snapshot of women's living conditions using recent worldwide data. Be it biased sex ratios, child marriage, or gender-based violence, possible determinants and solutions are analyzed through the lens of the scientific literature presented in the following sections.

This Element more globally speaks to the role economic development plays in gender inequality. While economic growth itself can help countries improve gender equality by, for instance, facilitating a sectoral shift toward a generally more female-dominated service sector, targeted policies should provide a more comprehensive push toward women's empowerment. As will be shown at various occasions across this Element, many indicators of gender inequality report a negative trend with GDP per capita, giving the impression that, overall, women's conditions improve with a country's wealth. Yet, drawing particularly from evidence on son preference and gender-based violence, the reader will notice that discriminatory practices are still far from absent in rich countries. In societies with a preference for boys, sex ratios have become even more biased once access to sex-detecting technologies during pregnancy became widespread. Scientific evidence documents the existence of son preference in some rich countries (Dahl & Moretti, 2008) and its persistence even among immigrant communities in the host country (Abrevaya, 2009; González, 2018). Likewise, recent data document that women's victimization is far from eradicated in rich countries. Worldwide, adequate legislation against gender-based violence is still lacking, as only 12 countries have comprehensive laws that address all types and forms of violence against women (OECD, 2023).

The gender pay gap is still largely observed in both the public and private sectors of rich countries and parity in political representation at national parliaments is far from reached. Waiting for a trickle-down effect of economic growth to improve women's empowerment risks being deceiving and empirical evidence calls for targeted policies to end gender inequality.

The question then pertains to the effectiveness of policies for improving women's lives and achieving empowerment. The evidence reviewed in this Element encompasses policy reforms to ban discriminatory practices and grant equal rights to men and women, but also antipoverty programs, such as cash transfers, life skills and vocational training, and interventions aiming at facilitating women's access to formal education and to the labor market.[4] As it shall be discussed throughout this Element, some actions appear to be particularly effective, including banning child marriage, improving women's economic empowerment, and increasing girls' educational level. Other interventions, in turn, such as providing equal rights to inheritance, offering life skills and vocational training, or delivering unconditional cash transfers, present so far more mixed results and their design and implementation pose serious challenges depending on local constraints.

The legal reforms and societal changes Western countries – and several others – encountered during the twentieth century have greatly improved women's conditions and agency. Women are today legally free to choose and set their own lives. Rights, such as political rights, divorce, contraceptives, autonomously owning a bank account, and signing a work contract, are fairly recent achievements that date back to less than a century ago. Despite these dramatic improvements, worldwide most countries still legally discriminate against women and the great majority of the human population holds biased social norms and attitudes against women.

This Element questions the view that the structural transformation brought by economic development will be sufficient to eradicate gender inequality. Targeted policies granting equal rights and facilitating women's access to the labor market, along with a radical drift toward more progressive attitudes, behaviors, and social norms, are a pressing need to be addressed worldwide.

---

[4] The gender dimension is mainly analyzed in this study by focusing on women in the global South, even though it does not embrace a biological definition of gender as the sex (male/female) category does. The focus on women is mostly due to research in economics on LGBTQ+ people being still scarce, especially in the global South, despite these communities often facing significant challenges (Badgett, Carpenter, & Sansone, 2021; Button, Carpenter, & Feir, 2025).

2 Development and Gender Inequality: A Bidirectional Relationship

Arguably, the relationship between gender equality and development goes in both directions, and both directions matter for policymaking (Duflo, 2012; World Bank, 2012; Jayachandran, 2015). Development can decrease gender inequality, as higher incomes, better institution quality, and improved service delivery could enhance women's empowerment by facilitating access to health care and education, creating new job opportunities, and promoting equal rights. Gender equality also matters in its own right and is a core objective in itself. Besides, it is likely to increase efficiency, being beneficial to a wide range of societal outcomes. Granting, for instance, equal access to the labor market would substantially increase the labor force. And equal access to education would improve labor allocation, increasing productivity and, more broadly, enhancing a society's human capital, with benefits spanning from labor productivity to health and economic development. In sum, closing the gender gap could boost development at large.

2.1 Gender Inequality

Despite recent progress in women's life expectancy and education, their socioeconomic outcomes are still today systematically worse than men's across all countries in the world. Gender gaps persist in a variety of domains, including labor market participation, income, political representation, and legal rights. These gaps are especially large in developing countries.

To get a sense of the magnitude of gender inequality, the Gender Inequality Index (GII) developed by the United Nations Development Program provides a useful cross-country comparable metric. The index covers 193 countries and it is a composite measure accounting for gender inequalities in three domains: reproductive health, empowerment, and the labor market.[5] High values indicate high inequality between women and men. Importantly, the GII captures gaps between women and men in the same country, providing a measure of women's conditions relative to men's in a similar context – except for the reproductive health dimension. In other words, it shows the loss in potential human development due to inequality between women's and men's outcomes in these three dimensions.

---

[5] The reproductive health domain is measured by the maternal mortality ratio and the adolescent birth rate, the empowerment rate is measured by the share of women with at least secondary education and by the share of parliament seats held by women, and the labor market domain is measured by female labor force participation.

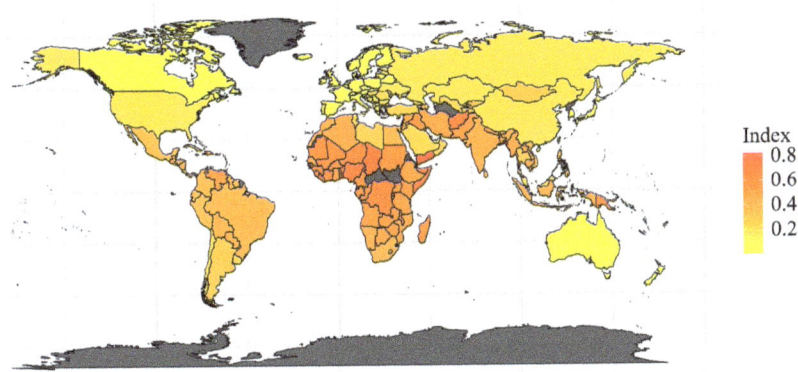

Figure 1 Gender Inequality Index (2022).
Notes: Author's calculation based on data from the Human Development Report (2022). The Gender Inequality Index is a composite index ranging from 0, where women and men fare equally, to 1, where one gender fares as poorly as possible in all measured dimensions.

The good news is that gender inequality decreased between 1990 and 2022, as shown by the GII values dropping from 0.579 in 1990 to 0.462 in 2022, corresponding to a 20% decrease relative to the 1990 level.[6] This progress was achieved mainly thanks to a considerable improvement in the reproductive health domain, with a stark decrease in the maternal mortality ratio and in the adolescent birth rate. Empowerment – measured by the share of seats in parliaments held by women and by the share of women with secondary-level education – has made some progress. The share of female members of parliament increased from 11.5% to 26.2%, a large change in relative terms, but still way below parity. The gender gap in secondary education is almost closed, as it dropped from 8.5% to 6.8%. In the past 30 years, the share of girls with secondary education has been multiplied by 1.8 and the share of boys by 1.5. The only indicator for which we observe a reversal trend is female labor force participation, which has, in fact, *decreased* since 1990, passing from 51% to 46.8%, leaving a gender gap in the labor market of 27.1 percentage points.

Despite these long-term improvements, the GII has stagnated since 2019, and the world is off track for achieving gender equality by 2030. A visual overview of gender inequalities is provided in Figure 1, illustrating the geographical distribution of the GII. Larger gender inequality persists in low-income

---

[6] The GII scores range from 0 to 1, with 0 indicating that women and men fare equally and 1 indicating that one gender fares as poorly as possible in all measured dimensions.

regions – mostly in Sub-Saharan Africa, Latin America, and South Asia – relative to high-income regions, such as Western Europe and North America.

Looking at past trends from 1990 onward reveals, however, important progress across all regions in decreasing gender inequality. The largest decrease is observed in South Asia, Latin America, and the Caribbean, where the GII dropped, respectively, by 32% and 30% relative to the 1990 level, scoring according to the most recent available data (2022) at 0.478 and 0.386, well below the world average. Progress also occurred in the Arab States, where the GII decreased by 23% relative to the 1995 level, scoring today at 0.523, and in East Asia and the Pacific, where the GII is today 18% lower than it was in 1998, scoring today at 0.340. Since 2019, however, progress has stagnated across all regions, apart from South Asia and Sub-Saharan Africa.

A similar picture emerges from the Global Gender Gap Index (GGGI), documenting gender inequality across four dimensions (economic participation and opportunity, educational attainment, health and survival, and political empowerment) across 146 countries (101 since 2006). The GGGI can be interpreted as the distance covered toward parity, that is, the percentage of the gender gap that has been closed. By 2024, at the world level, 68.5% of the gender gap was closed. That is 0.01 percentage point more than the previous year, a small improvement symptomatic of the stagnating situation occurring over the past 10 years. At the current rate of progress, it is estimated that parity will be achieved 134 years from now. Yet the world is not equally far from parity across the four dimensions included in the index. The Health and Survival gender gap has closed by 96%, the Educational Attainment gap by 94.9%, the Economic Participation and Opportunity gap by 60.5%, and the Political Empowerment gap by 22.5%. This means that parity in the Educational Attainment subindex will be achieved in 20 years' time, whereas it will take 152 and 169 years to achieve parity in the Economic Participation and Opportunity subindex and in the Political Empowerment subindex, respectively.

Progress in closing the gender gaps across these four dimensions has been uneven across the panel of 101 countries followed since 2006. Despite being still far from closed, the Political Empowerment gap reports the most significant shift, where parity has jumped a total of 8.3 percentage points to 22.8% since 2006. Notwithstanding this remarkable positive trend, no progress was observed since 2015, apart from a small improvement in 2020. Small progress was also observed over the past 20 years for the Economic Participation and Opportunity gap and in the Educational Attainment gap, for which parity has gained 4.8 and 4.2 percentage points, respectively. Yet the timeline to achieve parity in the Educational Attainment subindex stretched in the last year from 16 to 20 years due to a drop in girls' literacy rate and primary and tertiary education enrollment. Finally, despite the gender gap in the Health and Survival subindex being almost closed, it has, in fact, showed a downward trend since 2006 (–0.2 percentage points), dropping to its lowest level in 2022 (95.6%). The timeline to achieve full parity in this domain remains undefined.

Current levels and past trends in closing the gender gap appear uneven also across regions. The overall gap closed today by the countries in the global South is below 70%, the region with the lowest parity score being the Middle East and North Africa (MENA) (61.7%). The MENA region is also the one with the lowest level of parity in terms of Political Empowerment (10.8%), well below the world average of 22.5%. The Economic Participation and Opportunity index scores the lowest in South Asia (38.8%), also in this case well below the world average of 68.5%. Sub-Saharan Africa, in turn, performs better than the world average in all subindexes except for Educational Attainment, closing the gap by 86.7%, below the world average of 94.9%.

Looking at progress toward closing the gender gap across regions shows that the overall rate of progress has been the highest in Latin America and the Caribbean, where it has improved by 8.6 percentage points since 2006. Sub-Saharan Africa and the MENA region had stable progress, averaging 5.6 and 3.9 percentage points. South Asia is the only region where performance declined in the past 10 years, mostly due to a worsening of the Economic Participation and Opportunity subindex. Despite substantial progress toward gender parity till 2016 observed in this region, gender gaps have widened since then, resulting in a progress rate of 7.1 percentage points for the period 2006–2016 but of 3.9 percentage points for the period 2006–2024.

Today, gender inequality remains widespread, especially in the global South. While Latin America and Sub-Saharan Africa have made remarkable progress toward gender parity, the MENA region and South Asia exhibit much slower progress, especially in the past few years. Worryingly, the initial progress made in the 1990s and beginning of the twenty-first century seems to be stagnating since 2019, or even since 2016 in some cases. Large disparities persist in women's access to economic activities and to political participation, with most countries in the global South far away from achieving parity. These patterns across the world pave the way for the bulk of recent scientific analysis in economics looking for solutions to address gender inequalities.

2.2 Discriminatory Social Institutions and Gender-Biased Attitudes

The persistence of gender inequality and its negative association with development are well exemplified by the degree to which unequal opportunities and

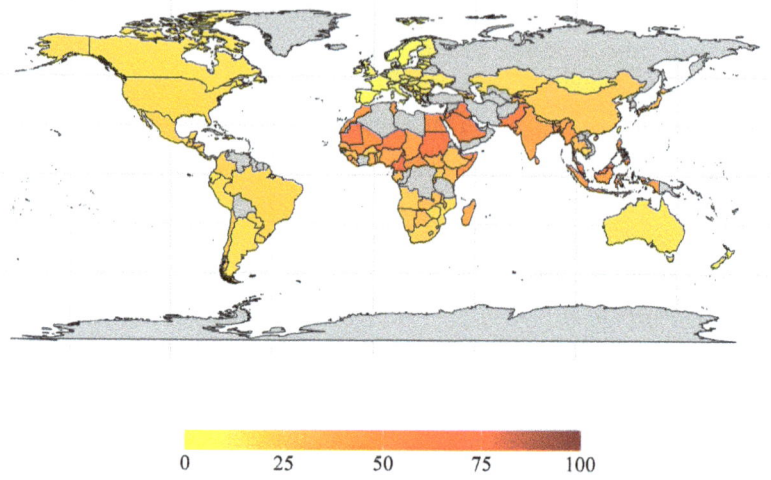

Figure 2 Social Institutions and Gender Index (2023).
Notes: Author's calculation based on the OECD Gender Institution and Development dataset (2023). The Social Institutions and Gender Index (SIGI) is a composite index measuring discriminatory social institutions across 179 countries, ranging from 0 to 100, with 0 indicating no discrimination and 100 indicating absolute discrimination against women. It is calculated by first computing subindices for each of the four categories of variables presented in the table, which are then averaged with equal weighting to obtain the final index.

rights are embedded in the legal and institutional framework. Still nowadays, we observe persistent discriminatory laws, social norms, and practices, such as restricted women's rights and civil liberties, that are among the main root causes of gender inequality.

Recent data about discriminatory social institutions are gathered by the Social Institutions and Gender Index (SIGI), providing information at the country level on four dimensions: discrimination in the family, restricted physical integrity, restricted access to productive and financial resources, and restricted liberties. The most recent data show that worldwide 40% of women and girls reside in countries where social institutions exhibit high or very high levels of discrimination against women (OECD, 2023). Fundamental rights, including the right to work, are at risk and have already been legally restricted in multiple countries. A first glance at Figure 2 reveals that West and East African countries, as well as Middle Eastern countries, are characterized by more discriminatory social institutions than the rest of the world. While in the MENA region no country reports a low discrimination level of social institutions, in the African continent only four countries do (Ivory Coast, Mozambique, Rwanda, and Zimbabwe).

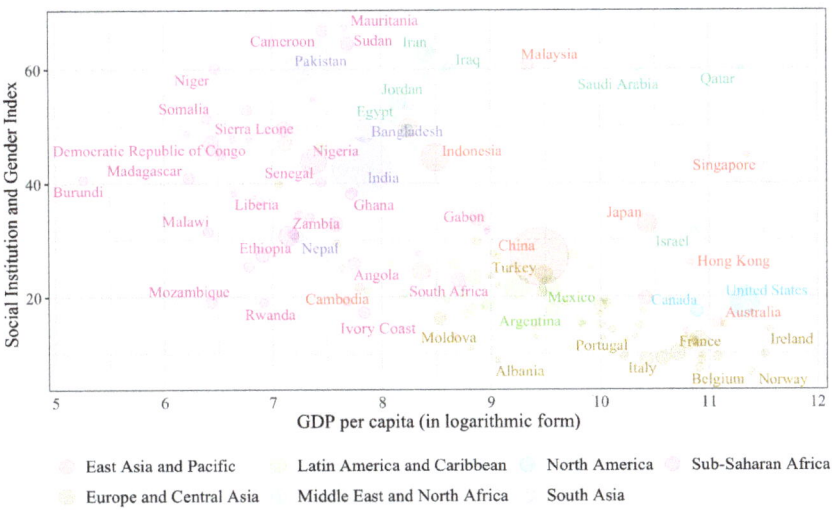

Figure 3 GDP per capita and the SIGI (2023).

Notes: Author's calculation based on the OECD Gender Institution and Development dataset (2023). GDP per capita is gross domestic product divided by midyear population size. Data are in 2023 US dollars from World Bank national accounts data and OECD National Accounts data files (2023). For more information about the Social Institutions and Gender Index see notes of Figure 2. Size of circles relates to country's population size.

Crossing information about the SIGI with GDP per capita shows an overall negative trend, whereby social discrimination is less pronounced in richer countries (Figure 3). Despite this general cross-country negative trend, there are, however, important exceptions among both rich and poor countries. Saudi Arabia and Qatar, together with other Middle Eastern countries, stand out for persistent laws and attitudes biased against women, despite a high level of GDP per capita. At the other end of the GDP distribution we also observe a variety of situations. Poor and middle-income countries exhibit various degrees of social discrimination against women, with some poor countries having a similar discrimination level as rich countries, despite their fewer economic resources. For instance, countries like Ivory Coast and Rwanda report a similar level of gender discrimination as Canada and the United States of America, despite a level of economic development similar to that of Bangladesh or Pakistan, where the SIGI is, however, three times larger.

An insightful perspective is offered by looking at the single dimensions contained in the SIGI (Table 1). While discriminatory laws are most present in low-income countries, we observe that worldwide laws regulating family affairs, access to abortion, access to work, and protection against violence are

Table 1 The Social Institutions and Gender Index across countries' income groups

	World	Low income	Lower middle income	Upper middle income	High income
Discrimination in the family subindex (0–100)	37.77	54.73	52.15	32.84	25.22
Share of countries where:					
Women do not have the same right as men to be either "head of household" or "head of family" and/or to be legal guardians of their children	32.95	58.33	37.50	23.40	26.32
Women do not have the same right as men to divorce	42.61	66.67	58.33	34.04	26.32
Women do not have the same right as men to inherit	23.30	29.17	39.58	17.02	12.28
Child marriage is legal	17.05	25.00	25.00	8.51	14.04
Restricted physical integrity subindex (0–100)	27.21	31.77	32.35	26.47	21.25
Share of countries where:					
The law doesn't protect women against violence	37.50	50.00	43.75	34.04	29.82
The law doesn't protect women and girls from female genital mutilation	11.93	20.83	14.58	10.64	7.02
The law doesn't always protect women's right to a legal and safe abortion	46.59	54.17	62.50	48.94	28.07
Access to productive and financial assets subindex (0–100)	27.05	43.39	38.85	23.19	14.63
Share of countries where:					
Women do not have the same right as men to own, use land assets, and/or make decisions over land	6.82	20.83	10.42	2.13	1.75

Women do not have the same right as men to open a bank account	2.27	8.33	4.17	0.00	0.00
Women do not have the same right as men to enter all professions, to work the same night hours, or to work or register a business without permission	43.75	62.50	58.33	44.68	22.81
Women do not have the same right as men to acquire, change, or retain their nationality	18.18	29.17	27.08	8.51	14.04
Restricted civil liberties subindex (0–100)	**26.49**	**34.80**	**34.78**	**21.98**	**21.47**
Share of countries where:					
Women do not have the same right as men to vote or to hold public and political office	2.27	4.17	2.08	0.00	3.51
Women do not have the same right as men to apply for national identity cards or passports, and/or to travel outside the country	16.48	25.00	20.83	14.89	10.53
Women's testimony does not carry the same evidentiary weight as men's testimony	13.07	29.17	12.50	8.51	10.53
Social Institutions and Gender Index (0–100)	**29.34**	**40.65**	**40.29**	**25.11**	**18.21**

Notes: Author's calculation from the OECD Gender Institution and Development data (2023). See notes of Figure 2 for more information on the Social Institutions and Gender Index.

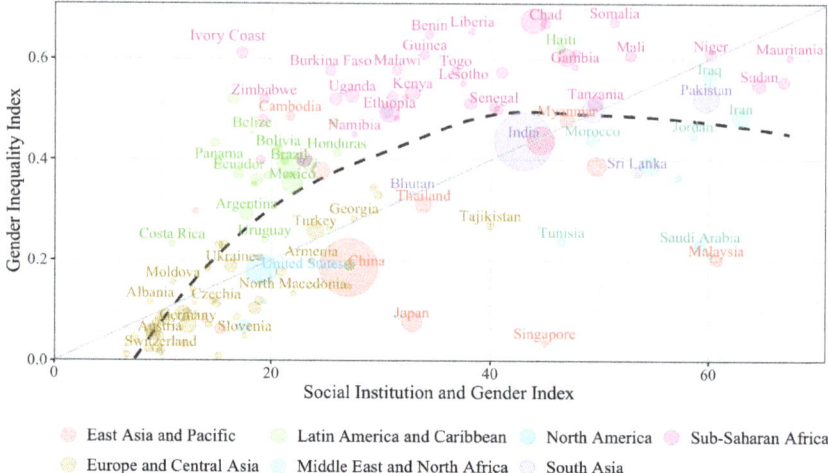

Figure 4 Gender Inequality Index and Social Institutions and Gender Index.

Notes: Author's calculation based on the Gender Inequality Index data reported in the Human Development Report (2022). The dashed line reports a nonparametric estimate of the cross-country relationship between the Gender Inequality Index and the Social Institutions and Gender Index. For more information on the Gender Inequality Index see notes of Figure 1. For more information about the Social Institutions and Gender Index see notes of Figure 2.

the ones most commonly discriminating against women. Strikingly, one out of two low-income countries does not legally protect women against violence and more than half do not grant equal divorce rights or equal right to work. In contrast, the right to open a bank account and equal political rights appear to be the ones granted by most countries across the world – and this despite the fact that worldwide only 27% of members of parliaments are women, such that at the current pace it will take at least 40 years to reach parity in national parliaments (OECD, 2023).

Discriminatory social institutions are part of the reason for large gender-gaps in education, income, wages, access to health services, and so forth. Crossing information of the GII and the SIGI shows a positive correlation between the two (Figure 4), whereby countries with a higher level of discrimination in their social institutions are also countries where gender inequality is higher. The pattern is, however, not linear. In the bottom left part of the graph, European and Central Asian countries together with North America report the lowest level of both gender discrimination (0 < SIGI < 20) and inequality (< 0.2). Yet, for low levels of social discrimination (20 < SIGI < 30) most countries exhibit a considerably higher level of gender inequality, close or above to 40%, with some countries even bypassing the world average of 0.46. As the

45-degree line shows, there are few exceptions where social discrimination is, in fact, higher than gender inequality. This suggests that, while discrimination in the legal and institutional framework is associated with gender inequality, most likely it is not the only factor explaining cross-country differences. Removing legal barriers to equal opportunities may help in achieving higher equality, but other factors, for instance discrimination rooted in biased social norms and attitudes, might be a persistent and relevant setback toward gender equality.

In fact, discrimination against women in terms of family rights, civil liberties, physical integrity, and access to productive and financial assets often goes hand in hand with gender-biased social norms and perceptions in the population.

The Gender Social Norms Index provides a general overview of gender-biased perceptions across the world population. Recent data, covering 85% of the global population, reveal that close to 9 out of 10 men and women hold biased views against women. Nearly half the world's population believes that men make better political leaders than women do, and 2 out of 5 people believe that men make better business executives than women do. Even in countries with the fewest gender biases, more than a quarter of people have at least one bias (UNDP, 2023). These biases hold across regions, income levels, and cultures and are incredibly persistent over time.

Looking at data from the World Value Survey based on a panel of 38 countries – accounting for 50% of the world's adult population for which attitudinal data are available for both wave 6 (2010-14) and wave 7 (2017–2022) – shows a stagnating situation. The share of people with no gender bias barely increased from 13% to 15.4% since 2010. Strikingly, these numbers are quite close for men (from 10.5% to 13.4%) and for women (from 15.5% to 17%), revealing how deeply rooted discriminatory social norms are in the world population.[7] Similarly, the share of people with at least one bias decreased modestly, from 86.9% to 84.6%, the most common bias relating to women's physical integrity (justification of domestic violence and abortion).

Looking at changes in the Gender Social Norms Index single dimensions reveals a more mixed picture. While justification for domestic violence has decreased by 12 percentage points, abortion is seen as not justifiable by 1 percentage point more of the respondents. Discriminatory attitudes toward women's leadership in politics and in the economic sphere have decreased by 4 and 6 percentage points, respectively, even though opinions about women holding equal rights and equal ability to work as men have worsened. Between

---

[7] Looking at data from wave 5 (2005–2009) – covering 32 countries – reveals similar figures. The share of women (men) without any bias corresponded to 16.5% (10.8%).

2014 and 2022, the share of individuals thinking that men should have more right to a job than women when jobs are scarce increased by 4 percentage points. Likewise, the share of the population thinking that it is almost certain to cause problems if a woman earns more money than her husband went up by 6 percentage points.

The presence of biased attitudes is stronger in countries with a high level of social discrimination, relating to the role social contexts play in shaping people's attitudes. Beliefs and attitudes are shaped by interactions with people and institutions play an important role in the persistence of social norms. When laws and policies allow for discrimination, similar practices will be found at home, at school, and in the workplace. Discriminatory laws and institutions also make it difficult for women to challenge prevailing social norms. Discriminatory institutions and social norms are an important challenge to women's empowerment and to the fight against gender inequality. Tackling discriminatory social institutions and regressive social norms remains a global top priority and has become the object of a recent literature in economics, representing a promising future research avenue.

2.3 Development and Female Labor Force Participation

The question of whether development enhances women empowerment has at first been analyzed by the economic literature in light of the trend of female labor force participation at different stages of a country's development. The main drivers of women's labor supply are usually identified by the standard economic theory with the opportunity cost of women's time and with the earnings of the other adult household members. The former implies that a higher wage will make work outside of the home more attractive – substituting away from housework – but it will also have an offsetting income effect, decreasing labor supply. The latter implies that the earnings of other adult household members will have an income effect on women's labor supply, decreasing female participation in the labor market.[8] The key question is whether these factors are affected by economic development.

Arguably, development may decrease female labor force participation (FLFP) if it is limited to raising men's productivity. In a context of gender-segregated sectors, if the male-dominated ones are the driving force of economic growth, women's participation in the labor force is expected to decrease

---

[8] Women's participation in the labor market may face additional constraints, including (but not exclusively) social norms about "acceptable" jobs for women outside of the home, off-household jobs being often less compatible with at-home child-rearing (Boudet, 2013). In addition, labor markets may not be fairly competitive, further restricting women's access.

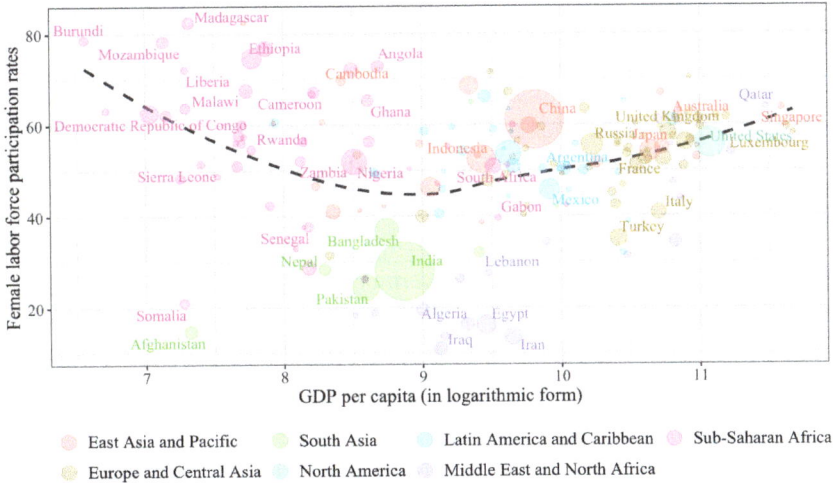

Figure 5 Female labor force participation and GDP per capita.

Notes: Author's elaboration based on data from World Bank gender data (2023). Female labor force participation measures the proportion of the female population aged 15 and older that is economically active during a specific time period. For more details about the GDP per capita measure, see notes of Figure 3. The dash line reports nonparametric estimates of the cross-country relationship between female labor force participation and GDP per capita. Size of circles relates to country's population size.

relative to men's. Development may, in turn, increase FLFP if women's wages rise at least as much as men's wages. This can occur if, for instance, female-dominated sectors drive or substantially contribute to economic growth. The order in which men's opportunities improve compared to women's significantly influences how FLFP evolves with development.

The relationship between development and FLFP is probably best exemplified by the U-shaped relationship detected by Goldin (1994) for 1985 and expanded by Mammen and Paxson (2000) to 1970, 1975, and 1980. Using data from 2022 from the World Bank, I report a similar U-shape relationship across all countries in the world in Figure 5. This figure shows that in very poor countries women are active in the labor market, with participation rates above 50%. These are mostly African countries where women work in family enterprises employed in low-wage and low-skill work activities, mostly informal and in the agricultural sector.

As countries get wealthier, women exit the labor market, partly because of the rise in men's market opportunities and partly because of increasing social barriers. Development at this stage is usually seen as driven by the manufacturing sector, most often precluded to (married) women. This gender segregation can be partly due to social norms about "acceptable" jobs for married women – despite it being quite common for unmarried women to work in factories. Possibly the stigma put on husbands who let their wives work in factories plays a role too, as no stigma is usually attached to white-collar jobs that require higher education levels. Another reason for women exiting the labor market at this stage of development might be the low wages offered by blue-collar jobs that do not compensate for the opportunity cost of working outside of the home. In this part of the U-shaped curve participation rate gets down to 20–30%, concerning mostly South Asian and MENA countries (Figure 5).

As countries continue to develop, women's education rises, pushing women back into the labor force as paid employees in white-collar jobs, such as services. Thanks to their increased education level and to social norms designating as "acceptable" for women jobs in the service sector, FLFP goes up again. This is often echoed by a decline in fertility rates and by less labor-intensive domestic work. Most countries in this part of the curve are found in East Asia, Latin America, Europe, and North America. An exception here is represented by Qatar, where FLFP rates are much higher than those in the MENA region and even higher than those of most other rich countries. Overall, higher levels of development, measured by the GDP per capita, are clearly associated with higher women's participation in the labor market.

The U-shaped pattern is found not only across countries, but also within countries when comparing households of different wealth levels. Recent work by Bandiera et al. (2022) explores the relationship by FLFP and GDP per capita by looking at five different household wealth quantiles across 115 countries since 1990. The study illustrates that the U-shape pattern is present across all wealth quantiles, but it is starker among poor women. Distinguishing between unpaid and paid work, the authors detect a similar U-shape curve also for paid work but only among women in the poorest quantile. While the prevalence of unpaid work declines for all as countries get richer, with men and women from richer households substituting unpaid work for paid work, in contrast, women from poorer households "disappear" from the measured labour force, generating the U-shape pattern. This is unlikely to be explained by poorer women consuming more leisure – as richer women, who can afford more leisure, do not disappear from the labor force. Another possible explanation is that poorer women quit unpleasant occupations or have to dedicate more time to domestic unpaid work as countries get richer.

Focusing on Africa, the shift of the female labor force from agriculture to the service sector explaining part of the U-shape relationship was found to take place since the 1970s (Dinkelman & Ngai, 2022).[9] Data from 2011 confirm that African countries are on the declining part of the U-shape curve. Yet, for some North African countries the FLFP takeoff observed by Mammen and Paxson (2000) at a GDP per capita of $10,000 does not seem to occur. Tunisia, Morocco, and Algeria present among the lowest FLFP rates, despite their middle-income status. This contrasts with other countries of similar income levels, such as South Africa, Gabon, and Namibia, where the rate of FLFP is about double.[10]

This is not to say, however, that high FLFP rates always coincide with high levels of market work. The extensive margin of work activity can, in fact, differ substantially from the intensive margin expressed by the number of work hours. In other words, despite a large share of active women, the amount of time spent in the labor market seems to remain limited. This can be partly explained by the large amount of household work performed by women, which is higher for women than men in every country of the world, and especially large in low and middle-income countries. In this respect, it is worth mentioning that nowhere in the world do men and women contribute equally to unpaid care work. Worldwide, women carry out two-thirds of all unpaid care work, spending on average about three times more time than men on these tasks.[11]

Distinguishing between the intensive margin in household work and in market work, a negative relationship appears between development and weekly hours of female household work (Bridgman, Duernecker, & Herrendorf, 2018), whereas the relationship is positive between development and female market hours. While in the wealthiest countries men and women work similar total hours, in the poorest countries women work significantly more hours than men. This is mostly due to women devoting most of their time to home production at low levels of GDP per capita, as already noted by Boserup (1970).

---

[9] Barely 10% of the African female labor force is employed in manufacturing.

[10] Among the possible factors behind this divergent pattern is the level of discrimination in social institutions that keeps women out of the labor force. According to the SIGI, Tunisia and Morocco report a high level of discrimination, whereas South Africa, Gabon, and Namibia report a low-medium level.

[11] Worldwide, women invest more time in unpaid care than men, with the gap ranging from 1.7 times more in the Americas to 3.4 times in Africa, and as high as 4.7 times in the Arab States (Addati et al., 2018). Each day, women devote about 4 hours and 25 minutes to unpaid work compared to men's 1 hour and 23 minutes. Over the course of a year, this disparity amounts to 201 full-time workdays (based on an 8-hour day) for women, versus just 63 for men (Addati et al., 2018).

Even in countries where FLFP rates are high, such as Uganda, Ghana, and Tanzania, the number of hours women devote to housework is more than double the time they spend in the labor market. In these countries women work less than 25 hours per week in the labor market but at least 32 to 48 hours per week in home production (Dinkelman & Ngai, 2022). Besides, African women's work activities are mostly performed in low-skill, low-wage jobs, either on their own account or contributing to family work without any monetary remuneration. This makes the aggregate rate of FLFP hardly a good indicator of women's empowerment in such contexts.

2.4 Gender Inequality and Development

Notwithstanding the negative link between gender inequality and development being well established, estimating the causal effect of the former on the latter has proved much harder. Studies relying on cross-country comparisons face at least two main challenges. First, cross-country and temporal variation in gender inequality is likely to be endogenous to economic growth, which directly affects gender disparities. This raises an issue of reverse causality. For instance, we know that female education is higher in rich countries than in poor countries. While economic growth is fostered by a higher level of human capital of both men and women, richer countries can provide more schools and of better quality, facilitating universal access to education and closing the gender gap in education. Second, gender inequality is usually correlated with other factors that affect economic growth and that are possibly hard to observe, raising an issue of omitted variables bias. Factors like civil and political rights, quality of institutions, and so on likely boost economic growth while also decreasing gender inequality.

Although most cross-country studies tend to confirm the negative association between gender inequality and development or economic growth, a number of studies find opposite results (for a review see Bandiera and Natraj, 2013). Moreover, as illustrated by the analysis of female labor force participation and GDP per capita, the relationship can be nonlinear, complexifying standard empirical analyses.

The stringent requirements for achieving robust causal inference are often the main constraint to providing causal interpretation of findings coming from cross-country analyses. The answer to the question whether women's empowerment can enhance development is probably to be found at a more micro level where natural or policy experiments can be studied. The use of a microeconomic approach relying on data at the individual level allows for a more focused but methodologically robust answer. When it comes to the contribution of women's economic empowerment – such as female employment and economic activities – to human development, microeconomic evidence shows positive impacts. The recent review by Balasubramanian et al. (2024) shows that interventions supporting female work activities improve women's employment, income, and physical health, as well as household consumption, education and health expenditures, savings, and asset accumulation.

3 Son Preference

One of the probably most well-known consequences of son preference is represented by the 100 million missing women across China, India, and Sub-Saharan Africa (Sen, 1992). Despite women benefiting on average from a higher life expectancy than men, an excess female mortality is recorded in several developing countries where, from birth to old age, girls and women are outnumbered by men.

Women, when provided with similar nutrition and healthcare, tend to outnumber men, as the women-to-men ratio of 1.05 in developed countries shows. In Bangladesh, China, and West Asia, Amartya Sen estimated this sex ratio to be 0.94, pointing to a deficit of 11% and corresponding to about 100 million women "missing."

Following the analysis by Amartya Sen, looking at the evolution of sex ratios of births in China, India, and the rest of the world between 1960 and 2020 reveals an interesting pattern (Figure 6). Sex ratios started being skewed in the 1980s when technologies to detect a child's sex during pregnancy became available. These ratios became more and more biased in the following 20 years and especially in China. Since 2010 the trend has reversed and sex ratios are becoming less skewed both in China and in India.

The initial work by Amartya Sen has been further enriched by showing the different life's stages at which women disappear. According to Anderson and Ray (2010), 23% were never born essentially due to selective abortion, 10% died during early childhood due to "girl neglect," 21% encountered maternal mortality, and 38% died above the age of 60, mostly due to lack of resources during widowhood.

Son preference, as captured by female excess mortality, presents different patterns across countries. For instance, while the number and percentage of missing women in India and China are quite similar, their distributions across ages are quite different. The analysis by Anderson and Ray (2010) shows that in 2000 in China 37% of all missing women were explained by prenatal mortality – that is, selective abortion. In contrast, this phenomenon would

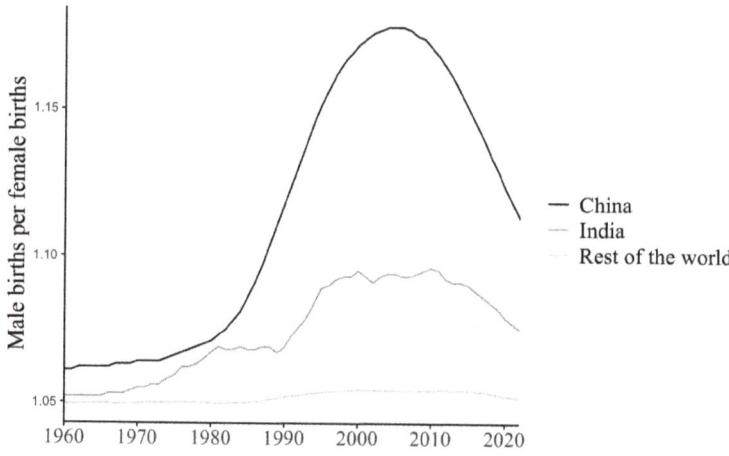

Figure 6 Trend of sex ratios at birth in China, India, and the rest of the world, 1960–2020.

Notes: Author's elaboration based on data from the World Bank, World Development Indicators.

concern "only" 11% of all missing women in India, while it seems still absent at that time in Sub-Saharan Africa. This is not to say, however, that there are no missing women in Sub-Saharan Africa. In fact, their share is higher than the share found in China or India: 47% against 31% in India and 34% in China. The pattern is, however, different in Africa, where women start "disappearing" at later ages. About 10.5% disappear during the first years of life, between 1 and 4 years of age. The largest share of missing women in Sub-Saharan Africa – about 51% of all missing women – appears between 20 and 40 years old, mostly due to the high rates of maternal mortality.

These different patterns across China, India, and Sub-Saharan Africa partly reflect the different ways in which parents have historically manipulated the ratio of surviving girls to boys by adopting reproductive behaviors such as the practice of son-biased fertility stopping, by neglecting female babies (short breastfeeding duration, lack of immunization, worse nutrition) or with sex-selective abortion once prenatal sex-detection technology became available.

3.1 Reasons behind Skewed Sex Ratios

Among the reasons for the existence and persistence of son preference, women's lower labor productivity relative to men's was proposed by Boserup (1970). According to this study, the gender gap in labor productivity would result from different farming systems, opposing the female to the male farming system. The former is characterized by shifting cultivation with an active and intense role of women. The latter is characterized by the use of the plough, employed by the men, to increase agricultural productivity. The male system, more capital intensive, reduces demand for labor, leaving little room for women's active participation and making them less valuable than men.

This hypothesis was formally tested – and confirmed – by Alesina, Giuliano, and Nunn (2013; 2018). In a similar vein, Carranza (2014) shows that variation in soil texture – determining the depth of tillage and hence the possibility to use the plough – explains the variation in sex ratios and FLFP across Indian districts. The larger the share of loamy soil allowing for deep tillage in a given district, the smaller the share of girls aged zero–six years old and of female agricultural workers.

The role played by the gender labor division in agriculture is similarly highlighted by Ebenstein (2021), who suggests that patrilineal land inheritance also contributes to biased sex ratios. Skewed sex ratios are indeed predominantly found among societies practicing patrilineal intensive agriculture, where land is passed to sons and never to daughters. Sex ratios are skewed mainly among parents without sons, while families with at least one son have balanced ratios. If son preference were due only to lower female productivity, skewed ratios would be present for all family sizes. Moreover, in societies with less land attachment, like "slash-and-burn" or nomadic cultures, sex ratios remain unbiased despite women's discrimination being present. Son preference would hence appear when parents intend to transmit their own (valuable) land to their offspring.[12] Patrilineality would be even stronger in places where capital investments – such as the use of the plough – make the land even more valuable.

The empirical analysis conducted by Ebenstein (2021) suggests indeed that countries having experienced earlier the Neolithic revolution – that is the start of farm agriculture – are more likely to be patrilocal and present today more skewed sex ratios.[13] Moreover, the author shows that in Sub-Saharan Africa patrilocal tribes exhibit higher sex ratios than nonpatrilocal ones living in the same country. While the causal interpretation of these results remains limited, an interesting pattern reveals that the divergence in sex ratios between patrilocal and nonpatrilocal tribes increases with children's age.

---

[12] It remains unclear why parents would prefer transmitting land to their sons and not to their daughters. The same reasoning could in theory hold for matrilineal societies. This is even more puzzling given that the author does not find a gender differential productivity in contributing to the household subsistence.

[13] This is also in line with the work by Hansen, Jensen, and Skovsgaard (2015) showing that today's cross-country variation in FLFP is partly explained by the timing of the Neolithic revolution.

This finding provides new insights against the common belief of son preference being absent in Africa, showing that, in fact, it manifests itself at later ages and mostly among patrilocal groups.

The importance of patrilineal land inheritance for the persistence of son preference is also highlighted by Bhalotra et al. (2019), who provide supportive evidence for the hypothesis that secured property rights in a patrilineal system reinforce son preference. The authors show that, following the land registration reform of West Bengal occurring after 1977, survival of boys in families without a firstborn son increased relative to those with a first son. In contrast, survival chances of daughters increased in families with a first son. This differential effect on survival of children depending on the firstborn sex is in line with a stark son preference attached to land inheritance.[14] Further analysis by Bhalotra, Brulé, and Roy (2020) shows that the 1976 Indian reform of land rights, aimed at providing women with equal rights to inheritance of ancestral property, resulted in an accrued son preference. Partly due to the stickiness of the patrilineality social norm, behaviors such as sex-selective abortions, girls' neglect, and fertility son-stopping are found to increase after the reform.[15] The 1976 Indian land reform has indeed proven to be ineffective at granting equal inheritance rights (Roy, 2015). Due to a persistent preference for boys, girls kept being excluded from accessing parental wealth (mostly land), which was transferred to sons by the mean of a testament, and were instead compensated with a larger dowry and by keeping them in school for longer.

Another possible reason for the persistence of son preference relates to the old-age support sons provide. As empirically shown by Ebenstein (2021), skewed sex ratios are predominantly found in patrilocal societies, where sons, but not daughters, remain living in their parents' house upon marriage. Further support for this hypothesis is provided by Ebenstein (2022), who shows that in China, South Korea, and Vietnam, where pension schemes expanded in recent years, the imbalance of sex ratios improved. Similarly, previous results by Ebenstein and Leung (2010) show that access to the pension system is associated with a lower imbalance of sex ratios following the expansion of the Chinese pension scheme. In line with this, households without any sons were more likely to engage in the pension program and to save more. These results confirm the hypothesis that son preference is – at least partly – shaped by the old-age support parents expect from their sons. As formal pension systems are established, the informal reliance on sons diminishes, and son preference along with it.

---

[14] Similar result is found by Almond, Li, and Zhang (2019) in the context of the 1978–1984 Chinese land reform, though the mechanism put forward by the authors in this case is not land inheritance, as landownership remained collective, but instead an increase in income.
[15] Similar results are found for the land reform occurring in West Bengal (Bhalotra et al., 2019).

A final note concerns evidence showing that sex ratios can become less biased when the returns to having a girl exogenously increase. Qian (2008) explores the effects of an increase in female-generated income versus male-generated income brought by an agricultural reform in Maoist China on girls' survival and educational attainment of boys and girls. She finds that after the reform girls' survival increased in tea-growing counties, where women had a comparative advantage in tea production and benefited from the increase in price brought by the reform. Similarly, the work conducted in India by Jensen (2012) shows that experimentally introducing labor-market opportunities for educated unmarried girls has positive spillovers on younger girls, increasing parental investment in their education and improving their health conditions.

Overall, the existence and persistence of son preference is documented in a variety of settings and its origins can be traced back to preindustrial societal determinants. Scientific literature seems to agree on three main factors: the historical gender gap in agricultural labor productivity, patrilineal land inheritance, and sons' old-age support. A still promising avenue for future research is to assess the capacity of policy reforms to divert this biased gender preference. Land reforms have proven so far inadequate, whereas pension schemes seem more effective, at least in countries with a tradition of sons' old-age support. Increasing the economic returns associated with having a daughter also seems to activate the right leverage. Further research could explore other types of policies acting on a similar trigger and implemented in contexts where son preference is still prevalent.

4 Child Marriage: Determinants and Policy Responses

Another stark dimension of gender inequality is the practice of child marriage, a human rights violation with profoundly negative consequences on a girl's life. Young married girls tend to drop out from school earlier, experience early pregnancy with possible negative health consequences, lack decision-making power at home, and are more likely to justify domestic violence and to be victims of intimate partner violence (Jensen & Thornton, 2003).

Every year on average 12 million girls marry under the age of 18. Across the world 640 million women have married before reaching adulthood, with South Asia accounting for almost half of child brides (290 million) (United Nations Children's Fund, 2023). Worldwide, one out of five women aged 20–24 was married under the age of 18. As Figure 7 shows, the largest prevalence of child marriage is found in the poorest countries, where two out of five women aged 20–24 were married by their 18th birthday. While in some contexts boys also happen to be married before adulthood, this phenomenon

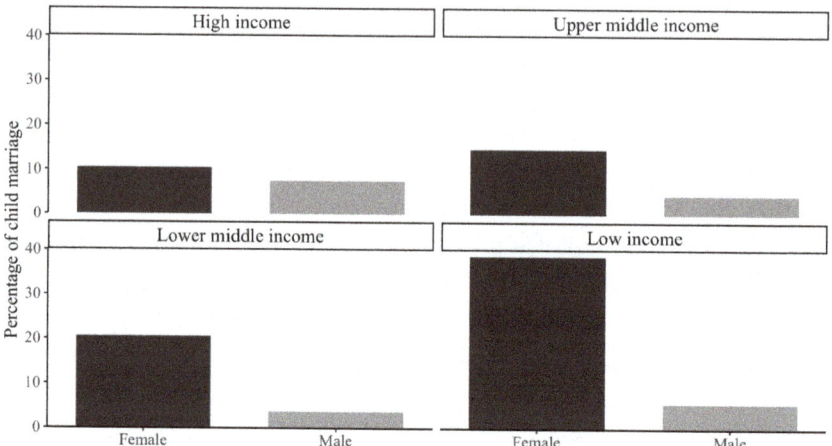

Figure 7 Prevalence of child marriage for girls and boys across countries' income groups.

Notes: Author's calculation based on data from the UNICEF 2015–2023. Country classification by income level based on the World Bank (2022–2023). The figure reports the percentage of women and men aged 20 to 24 years who were first married or in union before age 18.

concerns mostly girls. As Figure 7 shows, child marriage is not totally absent in richer countries. As we shall see, this is partly due to the existence of laws that allow for child marriage, most often with parental consent.

Figure 8 reports the 10 countries with the highest female child marriage prevalence rates in the world. They are all in Sub-Saharan Africa, except for Bangladesh. While in absolute numbers almost half of child brides are found in India, West and Central Africa report the greatest prevalence of child marriage (37%), followed by East and South Africa (32%), South Asia (28%), and Latin America (21%). Despite the prevalence of child marriage being halved in South Asia in the past 25 years, little progress has been made in the other regions. The reasons for the persistence of child marriage are complex and have made the object of a considerable literature, presented in the next subsection.

4.1 Determinants

The onset of puberty – age of menarche – is found to be an important determinant of child marriage, whereby girls' age of menarche varies between 11 and 16 years of age and influences the timing of parents' decision to marry off their daughters. Empirical evidence from Bangladesh (Field & Ambrus, 2008) shows that for girls aged 11–16 each additional year of delaying marriage increases the number of years of education by 0.22 and literacy by 5.6%. For each additional year of delayed menarche, a girl's marriage is

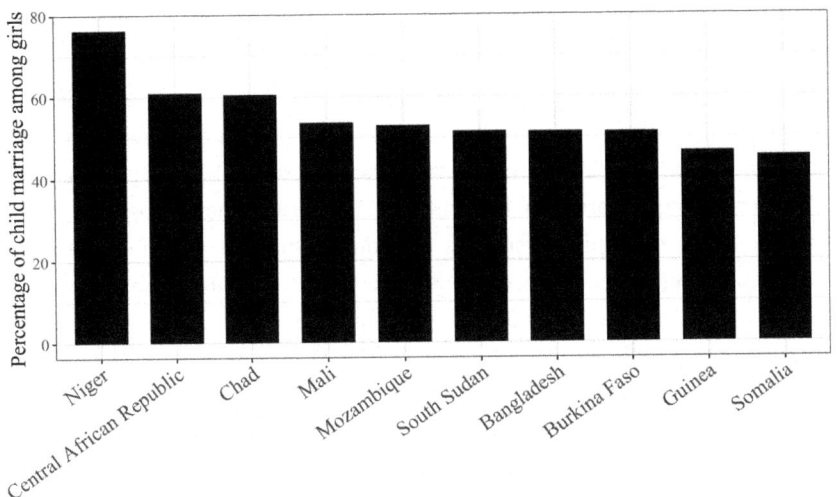

Figure 8 First 10 countries with the highest prevalence of female child marriage.

Notes: Author's calculation based on data from the UNICEF (2015–2023). Prevalence of female child marriage measured as the percentage of women aged 20 to 24 years old who were first married or in union before 18 years old.

deferred by 0.74 years. This not only affects girls' human capital accumulation, but also their health conditions, as girls marrying later are more likely to conduct prenatal checkups, to attend more antenatal visits, and to vaccinate against tetanus during pregnancy.

Also in the context of Bangladesh, one of the countries in the world with the highest rate of child marriage, Asadullah and Wahhaj (2019) explore the role played by the age of menarche in child marriage, using a within-household analysis that compares sisters living in the same household. The study confirms that the onset of puberty is a strong determinant of age of marriage and empirically shows that a one-year delay in menarche postpones marriage by half a year. As a result, girls stay in school for almost half a year more, hold less traditional views about gender norms, and their first childbirth is postponed by almost a year.

Additional evidence from India (Chari et al., 2017) shows the intergenerational benefits of delaying girls' marriage on child well-being. One year's delay in marriage increases the likelihood that children enroll in school (+3.1%) and that they complete the required vaccinations (+4.6%); it improves their weight-for-height z-score (+0.08) and their reading and math test scores. Besides, women marrying later are found to decrease their completed and desired fertility, partly thanks to a delayed age at first birth by about 0.8 years. In contrast, the authors find a negative effect on women's decision-making power concerning household decisions and on their freedom of movement outside of the home. As a main mechanism behind these intergenerational effects of delaying age of marriage, the authors point toward an age effect, whereby younger girls have lower status and bargaining power in the new household. The main results are indeed confirmed among a subsample of girls without education who got married before puberty. This brings the authors to exclude other possible mechanisms, such as the educational one – women marrying later stay longer in school, becoming more knowledgeable about childcare – and the spousal choice – women marrying earlier may end up in systematically different households.

While the onset of puberty can be seen as an idiosyncratic shock determining the age of marriage, recent evidence brings attention to the role played by negative aggregate household income shocks. Such negative shocks appear to matter for parents' decisions to marry off their daughters because child marriage represents one of the risk-coping strategies adopted by households against negative income shocks.

Recent work by Corno, Hildebrandt, and Voena (2020) studies the contemporaneous impact of droughts on child marriage across 31 Sub-Saharan African countries using data from 1994 to 2013 and in India using data from 1998. The authors show that women aged 12–24 experiencing a negative income shock – proxied by a drought – are *more* likely to get married in the same year by about 0.3 percentage points in Sub-Saharan Africa, whereas they are *less* likely to get married in India by 0.4 percentage points. Similarly, the likelihood of child marriage (girls marrying between 12 and 17 years old) increases by about 0.2 percentage points in Sub-Saharan Africa, while it decreases by about 0.4 percentage points in India.

The theoretical argument put forward by the authors to explain these divergent results between India and Sub-Saharan Africa lies in the different marriage payment transfer systems present in these contexts. In Sub-Saharan Africa, the large majority of ethnic groups practices brideprice, whereby the groom's family transfers a certain amount to the bride's family at the time of marriage. In India, instead, the most prevalent marriage payment system is the dowry, whereby it is the bride's family who transfers an amount to the groom or to his family. According to the authors, this creates a divergent system of incentives whereby, when a negative income shock occurs, households will delay or anticipate the marriage of their daughter. In a dowry system, the bride's family will prefer to delay marriage to consume the dowry today. In turn, in a brideprice system, the bride's family will prefer to proceed with their daughter's marriage to benefit from the transfer. Aggregate negative income shocks will likely also reduce the capacity for the groom to pay the brideprice.

The authors highlight, however, that under a patrilocal regime, the groom's family obtains support from the son and his wife, while the bridal family does not. Hence, despite the negative income shock, in a patrilocal brideprice system the groom's family will be better off with a marriage sooner than later. Yet, given the negative income shock, the brideprice amount will likely be lower than in normal times.

To test this theoretical explanation, the authors look at the impacts of droughts according to the prevalence of the brideprice system across different African ethnic groups. By splitting the sample based on the prevalence of brideprice at the group level, they confirm their main results when at least half of the ethnic group practices brideprice. The negative effect of droughts on child marriage found for India is also confirmed for Eritrea, a country where the dowry system is most prevalent.

4.2 Solutions

Among the possible policy responses to tackle child marriage, the literature analyzes two main broad types of intervention. One consists in the legal restriction banning child marriage, with laws setting the minimum age of marriage at 18. Another one is represented by interventions experimentally tested to impact child marriage – such as cash transfers (conditional or unconditional) and facilitating girls' access to the labor market – and by a wide array of gender-related policies – such as granting equal inheritance rights, facilitating access to contraception – and for which the impact on child marriage can be assessed.

4.2.1 Bans against Child Marriage

Since the 1948 United Nations' (UN) Universal Declaration of Human Rights the principle of granting equal marriage rights to men and women, respecting their free and full consent, has set the legal framework for banning child marriage and has been followed by subsequent international agreements. The 1962 UN Convention on Consent to Marriage, Minimum Age for Marriage, and Registration of Marriages and the 1979 UN Convention on the Elimination of All Forms of Discrimination Against Women require signatory nations to establish a legal minimum marriage age and ensure the registration of all marriages (United Nations, 1962; 1979). While the 1989 UN Convention on the Rights of the Child formally defines a child as an individual under the age of 18 (United Nations, 1989), it is the 1995 Beijing Declaration and Platform for Action that urged nations to enforce a legal minimum age for marriage, reaffirming 18 as the minimum age (United Nations, 1995). In 2016, the elimination of child

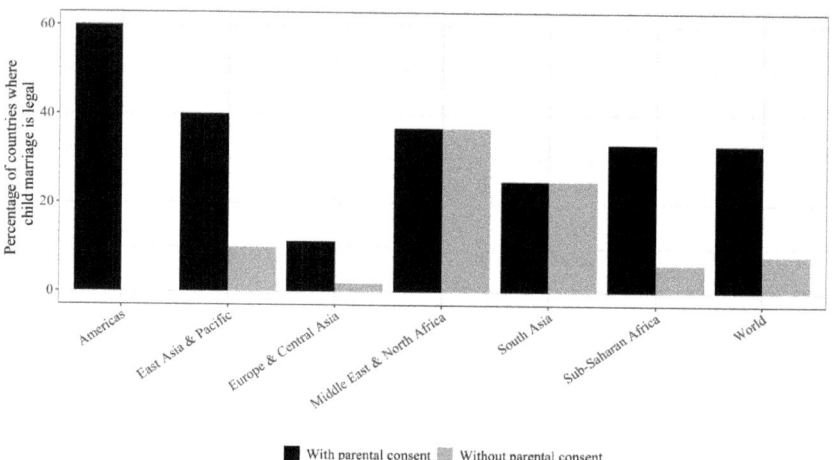

Figure 9 Share of countries allowing for child marriage, by macroregion.

Notes: Author's calculation based on data from the World Policy Center (2023). Child marriage is considered allowed when the minimum legal age of marriage for girls is 17 or younger.

marriage by 2030 became an international commitment under goal 5 on gender equality in the Sustainable Development Goals, resulting in a rapid increase in policy and programmatic efforts to end the practice.

In the past few years several countries introduced laws banning child marriage. While in 1995, more than 80% of countries allowed marriage for girls under 18 (with or without parental consent), by 2023 this rate had dropped to 33.16%. Yet, despite recent progress, according to the UN Children's Fund (2023), overall progress would need to be 20 times faster to end child marriage by 2030. Figure 9 shows that worldwide only 8.3% of countries – mostly in the Middle East, North Africa, Sub-Saharan Africa, and South Asia – allow for child marriage without parental consent for a girl to marry under 18 years old. The requirement of parental consent creates, in fact, a legal loophole to child marriage as most early marriages are arranged with parental involvement, but this does not grant any further child protection relative to countries where no legal parental consent is required.

Recent studies assess the effectiveness of child marriage bans across countries. Batyra and Pesando (2021) adopt a cross-national perspective comparing six low- and middle-income countries (Benin, Bhutan, Kazakhstan, Mauritania, Nepal, and Tajikistan) that raised the minimum age at marriage over the past two decades. They find the reforms were unsuccessful in decreasing child marriage. According to the authors, the level of enforcement remains weak, and legal exceptions based on parental consent and customary or religious laws remain in place.

The study by Collin and Talbot (2023) encompasses 90 developing countries between 1995 and 2012, out of which more than half did not have any legal ban against child marriage at the time of the study. The authors report a 60% prevalence rate of child marriage (legal and illegal) in 1980, which dropped by half in 2012. The main results, based on a cross-country and a within-country analysis, show poor law enforcement whereby legal bans were ineffective against child marriage. Adopting a regression discontinuity approach, the authors find that the age of marriage distribution does not show a discontinuity around the legal cutoff that we would expect if child marriage bans were effective. A weak law enforcement is found especially in rural areas.

Limiting the analysis only to 17 low-income countries that had already adopted a legal ban against child marriage, Wilson (2022) implements an event-study approach to investigate changes in child marriage associated with the timing of the legal ban across areas with different intensity levels of child marriage before the ban.[16] Among these selected countries more than one-third of female respondents were married before 18 years old, and among ever married respondents, the average age of first marriage was nearly 19 years old. The results show a 20% significant decrease in child marriage only in urban areas, but not in the overall sample or in rural areas. Additional results suggest that child marriage bans seem more effective at decreasing child marriage in countries with a preexisting legal minimum age of marriage (16 or 17 years old). Looking at specific age of marriage, the author finds that bans are particularly effective at discouraging child marriage of girls aged between 13 and 16 years old.

Child marriage bans also appear to improve the girls' lives in a variety of dimensions. Wilson (2022) observes a delay in the age of first birth (one standard deviation increase in ban intensity is associated with an approximately 0.42 year increase in age at first birth), the effect being larger in urban areas. There are positive effects also on the girls' number of years of education in urban areas only (+1 additional year) and on female labor force participation, both in urban and rural areas.

The study by McGavock (2021) similarly reveals heterogeneous effects of banning child marriage. Looking at the laws implemented across Ethiopia's semiautonomous regions, she finds a delay in women's marriage, in particular for girls under 16 by about 17% (6.8 percentage points) in areas where

---

[16] At the time of the study, 105 countries had a legal ban against child marriage. Wilson (2022) further restricts the sample to countries where the demographic and health survey data are available (60 countries). Out of these, the author selects only those countries banning marriage under the age of 18, irrespective of parental consent.

early marriage was more common prior to the reform. However, the effect of the reform, though larger, is insignificant among women belonging to ethnic groups with the strongest norms toward early marriage.

Overall these results highlight that banning child marriage can be a feasible solution, although in the absence of adequate enforcement, the law's impact remains limited and its effectiveness may vary across contexts. Among the various possible reasons for these mild effects is the presence of particularly tight social norms about age at marriage among some social groups, as the study by McGavock (2021) documents. The weak law enforcement may also reflect the presence of powerful elites opposing change in favor of gender equality and undermining the implementation of progressive policies (Robinson & Acemoglu, 2012; Kelsall et al., 2022). Exploring the reasons for this limited and heterogeneous effect seems a promising avenue for future research to assess the law's enforcement capacity under different local constraints.

4.2.2 Cash and In-Kind Transfers Conditioned on Girls Staying Unmarried

As documented by Corno et al. (2020) and Corno and Voena (2023) child marriage is (also) a risk-coping strategy whereby economically constrained households resort to marrying off their daughters in response to negative income shocks, essentially in societies practicing brideprice. This mechanism highlights the binding role of the monetary constraint, which is possibly linked to the lack of insurance and credit access as predominant market failure. A possible policy solution to address these constraints would then be to provide cash transfers to poor eligible households for them to avoid resorting to child marriage in the presence of a negative income shock.

One possible way for cash transfers to delay child marriage is by attaching the conditionality requirement to the girls staying unmarried. Empirical evidence testing for the effectiveness of this type of conditional cash transfers shows, however, mixed results. The study by Erulkar, Medhin, and Weissman (2017) evaluates the Berhane Ewhan multi-arm program that included transferring livestock to households under the condition of 12–17-year-old girls remaining unmarried and in school. The program was implemented across sampled communities in Ethiopia and Tanzania.[17] In Ethiopia, the main results show a one-tenth decrease in child marriage among girls aged 10 to 14 years old – but no effect for those aged 15 to 19 years old. In turn, in Tanzania the girls aged 15 to 17 years old saw their risk of ever being married

---

[17] The conditional asset transfer arm initially planned for a sample in Burkina Faso was then removed from the impact evaluation of the program due to design fallacy.

relative to the control group cut by half, though no effect was found on the 12–14-year-old girls.

The Apni Beti Apna Dhan (Our Daughter, Our Wealth) program implemented in the Indian state of Haryana consists in providing a financial grant transferred to households upon a daughter's birth, followed by a long-term savings bond redeemable by the unmarried daughter at the age of 18. Sinha and Yoong (2009) document the program's positive effects on the sex ratio and on girls' health - but not on education. A related study by Nanda et al. (2016) finds no significant decrease in child marriage, whereas they show that beneficiaries were more likely to marry at 18, probably using the cash transfer to fund their wedding.

A study by Buchmann et al. (2023) evaluates the impact of a multi-arm program implemented by the nongovernmental organization Save the Children in Bangladesh over two years (2008–2010). The program consisted of two randomized interventions: life-skills training conducted for six months at the community level and targeted at girls aged 10–19 years old and a conditional asset transfer consisting in cooking oil transferred every four months for two years to households with a girl aged 15–17 years old under the condition of the girl remaining unmarried. In a subset of communities the two interventions were provided simultaneously. The main results show a 4.9 percentage point decrease (equivalent to 16.7% relative to the control mean) in child marriage achieved by the asset transfer alone. This leads to an increase in the age of marriage by 0.21 years, suggesting that girls marry soon after their 19th birthday (average marriage age in the control group is 18.969). In contrast, the life-skills training, either alone or combined with the asset transfer, has no significant impact on child marriage. The authors explain their results with a theoretical model whereby delaying marriage is a negative signal of unobservable bride characteristics that grooms desire, such as docility and obedience, pushing all girls to marry earlier than preferred to avoid negative signaling. This makes the authors exclude the hypothesis that child marriage is due to financial constraints, as they do not observe any premium attached to higher age of marriage – such as higher dowry or lower groom quality.

4.2.3 Life Skills, Vocational Training and Job-Market-Related Interventions

Similarly to the work by Buchmann et al. (2023), several studies evaluate multi-arms interventions to test for the effectiveness of different approaches to fight child marriage.[18] Life-skills training is sometimes combined with

---

[18] For a recent review see Malhotra and Elnakib (2021).

vocational training or access to the labor market with the aim of tackling multiple pathways simultaneously. Life-skills training aims at avoiding child marriage by empowering the girls themselves, making them more capable of negotiating later marriages. This type of training is often coupled with community-level awareness campaigns to shift social norms. Meanwhile, improving the girls' job skills and facilitating their access to the labor market aims at providing a viable alternative to marriage, while at the same time enhancing the girls' financial autonomy, as household financial constraints are still often considered to drive child marriage decisions.

Work by Amin, Saha, and Ahmed (2018) evaluates the Bangladeshi Association for Life skills, Income, and Knowledge for Adolescents (BALIKA) program, whereby three different interventions targeted girls aged 12–18: an educational tutoring support, training for promoting gender rights awareness, and vocational training. In addition, all girls were offered a 44-hour life-skills training program over 18 months and an awareness campaign was conducted at the community level. Results show that all three interventions successfully reduce the risk of child marriage relative to the control group by about 25–30%.

A similar approach relying on training adolescent girls in "safe spaces" is adopted by the BRAC's Empowerment and Livelihood for Adolescent Girls (ELA) initiative. The study conducted by Bandiera et al. (2020) in Uganda targeted girls aged 14–20 who were offered life-skills training combined with vocational training. Despite a low attendance rate (21%), the intervention managed to decrease the likelihood of being married by 6.8 percentage points, a 50% reduction relative to the control mean. However more mixed results are found by two other studies evaluating the same intervention in different contexts.[19] No significant impacts are found on marriage and childbearing in Tanzania (Buehren et al., 2017) while an increase in marriage and childbearing rates is found in South Sudan (Buehren et al., 2017). Among the possible reasons discussed by the authors to explain these divergent findings stems the different context, different implementation teams, interventions implemented at different levels of scale, with different amounts of resources available. Besides, in the South Sudan intervention eligible girls were slightly older (15–24 years old). Finally, Boulhane et al. (2024) tested for the effectiveness of training girls aged 8–24 years old on life skills in safe spaces implemented in Ivory Coast. While the stand-alone intervention had limited impacts on girls' empowerment, it had the largest impacts when coupled with similar safe spaces for boys and men of the same age group. Despite encouraging effects on girls'

---

[19] A third study evaluates the same program in Sierra Leone during the Ebola outbreak (Bandiera et al., 2019); however, the authors do not report the effect on marriage.

sexual and reproductive health, economic activities, and decision-making, the study does not find any significant decrease in girls' marriage or pregnancy.

To discourage early marriage, another approach is to facilitate girls' direct access to the labor market. The intervention studied by Jensen (2012) tackles girls' access to the labor market by conducting information campaigns and recruitment initiatives in rural villages in the outskirts of Delhi. The intervention randomly assigned villages to be connected to recruiting services of business process outsourcing (BPO) industry – such as call centers and back-office services. The BPO industry represents a new fast-growing economic sector that employs mostly female workers with at least 10–12 years of schooling. The study finds that girls aged 18–24 years, mostly unmarried, are 4.6 percentage points more likely to be working for a BPO industry one year later. Interestingly, this impacts their family outcomes. Even though the age composition of the sample does not allow researchers to explore effects on child marriage, results show a decrease in the likelihood of being married and of childbearing by about 5 percentage points. The intervention has also positive spillovers on younger girls aged 6–17 who are 5 percentage points more likely to be enrolled in school, closing the educational gender gap relative to boys.

Similarly to the BPO industry, in Bangladesh the ready-made garment industry has spiked since the 1990s, accounting today for 75% of the country's export earnings. This sector offers a large-scale employment opportunity for women with basic literacy and numeracy. The study by Heath and Mobarak (2015) assesses the impact of the sector's expansion on women's family life by relying on retrospective data from households living in 60 Bangladeshi villages that vary with respect to their distance to garment factories, and to the date when the first factories opened close to each village. The authors show that girls living in villages close to a garment factory when aged between 10 and 23 years old – that is the window that covers most of the marriage age in the sample – are 13 percentage points more likely to work outside of the home and are 0.3 percentage points less likely to be married for the average number of years of exposure to the garment factory (6.4 years), corresponding to a decrease of 28% relative to the control mean. The effect sizes are the largest for girls aged 12–18. The likelihood of childbearing decreases too, by 0.23 percentage points, corresponding to 29% relative to the control mean.

The empirical evidence available to date seems to point toward girls' access to the labor market as the most effective policy against child marriage, with impact sizes similar to those of passing legal bans found by Wilson (2022). Evidence about life-skills and vocational training shows, in turn, more mixed results, making it hard to conclude whether this type of intervention is successful against child marriage. Divergent findings suggest that interventions of this type may be highly sensitive to context, implementation quality, and available resources. Moreover, girls are targeted at a relatively young age, most often before their 15th birthday, making parental permission and acceptability key for ensuring high participation rates. Provided the strong social norms about age at marriage, targeted training interventions may benefit from complementary community campaigns to grant a wider endorsement.

4.2.4 Education-Related Interventions

Another approach to tackle child marriage relies on education programs. In a similar spirit as providing job skills or facilitating access to the labor market, schooling programs aim at increasing girls' human capital or opportunities by making schooling a viable alternative to marriage. Schooling and marriage are often seen as mutually exclusive, such that for as long as girls stay in school their marriage is delayed (incarceration effect). Moreover, education might reinforce the girls' skills, confidence, and aspirations, making them able to negotiate a later marriage. Reaching a critical mass of girls enrolled in school – especially at the lower-secondary level – might also encourage a general shift in social norms by pushing parents to delay the marriage decision.

A study by Baird, McIntosh, and Özler (2011) evaluates the effect of providing a conditional cash transfer (CCT) versus an unconditional cash transfer (UCT) to girls aged 13–22 in rural villages of Malawi. The CCT was conditioned on the girls' school attendance, targeting girls already in school or who dropped out from school. In turn, the UCT provided cash without any condition and targeted only girls enrolled in school. Transfers took place over two years. At the end of the program, the CCT was found to be effective in increasing girls' school attendance and test scores. But it was only the UCT that was effective at decreasing the likelihood of marriage (by 8 percentage points, equivalent to a 44% decrease relative to the control mean) and childbearing (by 6.7 percentage points, corresponding to a 27% decrease relative to the control group).

This shows that while CCTs may have an indirect effect on marriage and childbearing through increased school participation, UCTs can have a direct effect through income. Conditionality was in this case effective for education-related outcomes, but it undermined social protection by denying support to households who could not comply (anymore) with the conditionality requirement. Nevertheless, these positive effects brought by the UCT were not sustained two years after the end of the program. As Baird, McIntosh, and Özler (2019) show, marriages and childbearing spike among UCT beneficiaries soon after the end of the program, leading to lower levels of empowerment compared with both the CCT and the control groups. In contrast, girls who were out of school at baseline and who benefited from the CCT reported lower marriage and pregnancy rates two years after the end of the program.

The lack of sustained effect of antipoverty UCT programs is also confirmed by Dake et al. (2018) who find no significant effects of a UCT implemented in Malawi and Zambia on early marriage of girls aged 14–21 years old. In turn, the capacity of CCTs and school subsidies to decrease early marriage and pregnancy by keeping girls in school is confirmed by other studies in several different contexts (Angrist et al., 2002; Duflo, Dupas, & Kremer, 2015; Amin et al., 2018; Hahn et al., 2018; Giacobino et al., 2024). This literature shows that, by keeping girls longer in school, marriage is delayed. The evidence showing long-lasting effects (see, for instance, Hahn et al., 2018) provides support to the hypothesis that education acts on the age of marriage not only through an incarceration effect – lasting for as long as the girl is in school but dissipating soon after – but as a transformative process that enhances girls' empowerment. An open question remains about the pivotal mechanisms that make CCTs successful at delaying marriage: whether they mostly act on the girls' side, by improving their human capital, financial autonomy, and decision-making power; whether they successfully shift social norms about age at marriage by reaching a critical mass of households; whether they act on the parents' side by increasing their perceived returns to girls' education; or whether they trigger some other type of mechanisms, or even a combination of all these. Currently, different studies point toward different mechanisms, as these may, in fact, vary with context and intervention design.

It is worth mentioning that the existing literature on educational programs addressing girls' outcomes, and more specifically child marriage, is limited to the demand side of education programs. That is, the focus is on providing households with cash transfers or other support programs for encouraging girls' enrollment and attendance. A yet unexplored but promising avenue of research is the analysis of supply-side interventions – for example, school building, improving school infrastructures, female teachers, content of curriculum, etcetera – on girls' outcomes.

Overall, school subsidies and conditional cash or in-kind transfers appear to be the most effective method for delaying marriage, more successful than family economic support, such as antipoverty UCTs. Facilitating access to the labor market also appears successful in delaying marriage and childbearing. The study by Jensen (2012) shows that providing household with concrete opportunities for their daughters' employability effectively shifts attitudes and behaviors, leading to intergenerational effects. In turn, enhancing girls' human capital, particularly through life skills, livelihoods, and gender rights training, shows more mixed results.

Besides their effectiveness, some of the interventions enhancing girls' human capital and work opportunities appear to be scalable. The studies by Jensen (2012) and by Heath and Mobarak (2015) shed light on the effects of women's employment in fast-growing economic sectors that operate nationwide, possibly impacting millions of women. While few studies report information about their cost-effectiveness and capacity to operate at scale, the Colombian government school voucher program (Angrist et al., 2002; Angrist, Bettinger, & Kremer, 2006) and the Bangladeshi government program for school support (Hahn et al., 2018) are examples of large-scale interventions that successfully reach vast numbers of girls and appear to be sustainable.

5 Gender-Based Violence

The persistent widespread prevalence of domestic violence is likely one of the best proofs of the lack of efficient allocation within the household. Violence against women was recognized as a human rights violation by the UN in 1992. It encompasses various forms of abuse, including economic, psychological, sexual, and physical violence, as well as practices such as female genital mutilation (FGM) and child marriage.

An estimated 30% of women worldwide have experienced intimate partner violence (IPV) or non-partner sexual violence (NPSV). This equates to 736 million women globally (WHO, 2021). On a global scale, 7% of women have been sexually assaulted by someone other than a partner. Additionally, 38% of murders of women are committed by an intimate partner and approximately 200 million women have undergone FGM.

The prevalence of IPV against women – be it over the life course or in the past 12 months – is higher in the global South than in the global North. In the least developed countries, 37% of women are victims of violence at some point in their life and 22% have been victims of violence in the past 12 months, against a global average of 27% and 13%, respectively. Across countries, the share of women who suffered from violence in the past 12 months is negatively correlated with a country's wealth (Figure 10). Yet even among rich countries IPV is not totally absent. Saudi Arabia, in particular, stands out as an outlier. Despite being a rich country, it reports the highest IPV prevalence rate in the world. This crude correlation should, however, not be given a causal interpretation, meaning that it is not (only) economic wealth that decreases IPV. Intimate partner violence is lower in richer countries for a whole lot of reasons. Wider societal and institutional changes accompanying economic development may contribute to a lower level of violence. Societies in wealthier countries usually report less discriminatory gender norms and a weaker acceptance of violence,

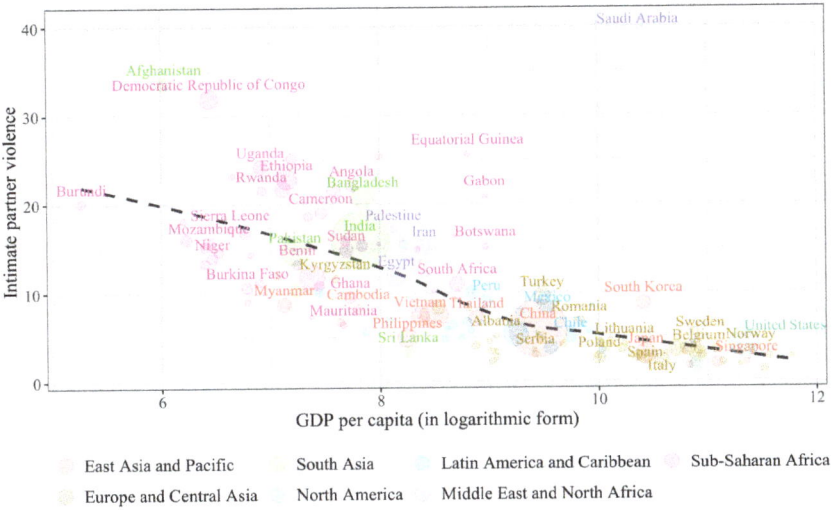

Figure 10 Intimate partner violence and GDP per capita.

Notes: Author's elaboration based on data from the OECD Gender Institution and Development Database (2023) and from the World Bank (2023). The dashed line reports a nonparametric estimate of the cross-country relationship between the prevalence of intimate partner violence and GDP per capita. Intimate partner violence is measured as the percentage of ever-partnered women and girls subjected to physical and/or sexual violence by a current or former intimate partner in the previous 12 months. For more details about the GDP per capita measure, see notes of Figure 3. Size of circles relates to country's population size.

and they tend to grant laws and institutions free from gender discrimination (Heise & Kotsadam, 2015).

5.1 Measurement of Gender-Based Violence

The available figures are likely only the tip of the iceberg. The measurement of gender-based violence (GBV) is particularly challenging partly because of a lack of available data until very recently. By 2010, only 82 countries provided survey data about GBV. This number rose to 161 in 2018. Notwithstanding, surveys still tend to differ in terms of questionnaires and methodologies, sometimes lacking comparability across countries.

Besides, accuracy of survey-based and administrative data can be limited. Women often underreport their experience of victimization due to factors such as trauma, shame, and fear of repercussions. Additionally, administrative data (police reports, court judgments, social services, and health statistics) significantly underreport the phenomenon because few women report violence to the authorities.

The risk of misreporting affects not only the measurement of victimization but also attitudes toward violence. Provided that talking about violence-related issues is a sensitive topic, respondents – either victims or perpetrators – may be reluctant to tell the truth. They may fear being judged, endangered, or legally penalized. Misreporting bias could lead to over- or underestimating prevalence of sensitive issues when using standard direct questions survey techniques. In response, a vast literature uses experimental surveys to accurately measure sensitive attitudes and behaviors.

The widespread female support for IPV in the global South, most often outnumbering male support (Cools and Kotsadam, 2017), is a puzzle possibly related to misreporting. Figure 11 shows that IPV justification is generally higher in countries with higher IPV prevalence, suggesting a likely bidirectional relationship partly influenced by misreporting. Widespread IPV acceptance likely sets the ground for an extensive use of domestic violence, being tolerated and assumed to be a common practice. Meanwhile, the large support for IPV might signal the desire to conform with a social norm perceived as predominant (Bertelli et al., 2024). In this respect, even victims may prefer to justify IPV to "rationalize" their own sufferings. While the internalization of discriminatory social norms may at least partly explain this pattern, it also raises the issue of correctly measuring victimization and attitudes. In Figure 11 we observe that IPV is always more justified than practiced (except for Saudi Arabia), somehow in line with the hypothesis according to which misreporting might affect negatively the report of victimization but positively its acceptance.

5.1.1 List Experiments

Among the experimental survey techniques used in the current literature to avoid the risk of misreporting, list experiments (LEs) have been widely adopted. Instead of directly asking respondents, LEs present them with a list of items and ask them the number of items they agree with. This survey technique is used in experimental surveys where respondents are randomly allocated to a control and a treatment group. In the control group, respondents are asked about a list of J "baseline" items, while in the treatment group, respondents are asked about a list of $J + 1$ items, with the additional item being the sensitive one related to the research topic. Since respondents are randomly assigned to the two groups, the prevalence rates of the baseline items should be the same across both groups. Therefore, the difference in the average number of items

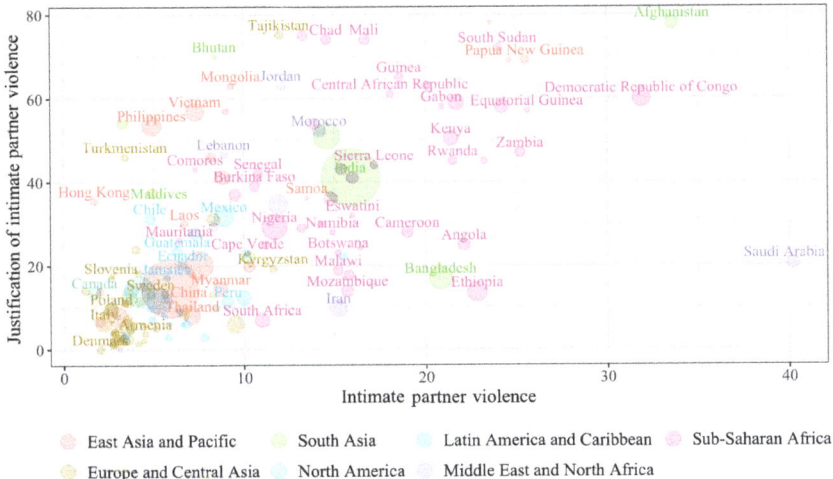

Figure 11 Intimate partner violence prevalence and justification.

Notes: Author's elaboration based on data from the World Value Survey (Waves 5–7, 2017–2022) and the OECD Gender Institution and Development database (2023). See Figure 10 for the measure of intimate partner violence (IPV). Justification of IPV is calculated as the share of girls and women aged 15 to 49 years who think a husband to be justified in hitting or beating his wife for at least one of the following reasons: if his wife burns the food, she argues with him, goes out without telling him, neglects the children, or refuses sexual relations. Size of circles relates to country's population size.

reported in the treatment group versus the control group serves as an estimate of the prevalence of the sensitive item in the sample.

In addition, in the control group respondents are asked about the sensitive item in a standard direct way. Two measures of the sensitive item prevalence rate can be computed: one from the LE, based on the comparison between the counts declared by respondents in the two groups; and one from the direct question administered to the control group. Any significant difference between the two prevalence rates should signal the presence of misreporting.

The use of an LE has the main advantage of avoiding any public disclosure of sensitive personal information, granting a higher confidentiality than standard direct questions and strongly limiting the risk of social desirability bias. The example reported in Table 2, taken from Bertelli et al. (2025), shows the structure of a typical LE compared to a standard direct question.

With regard to the practice of GBV, the existing literature shows that GBV victimization is often misreported – mostly underreported – by victims

Table 2 Lists and questions about gender-based violence
(adapted from Bertelli et al., 2025)

	Treatment group (LE)	**Control group (DQ)**
Baseline item:	– My parents always got along.	– My parents always got along.
Baseline item:	– In the evening, women are not safe in the street.	– In the evening, women are not safe in the street.
Baseline item:	– Corporal punishment should never be used in school.	– Corporal punishment should never be used in school.
Sensitive item:	– *A wife who does not respect her husband deserves to be hit.*	– *Does a wife who doesn't respect her husband deserve to be hit?*

when asked standard direct questions (Plummer et al., 2004; Phillips et al., 2010; Joseph et al., 2017; Bulte & Lensink, 2019; Traunmüller, Kijewski, & Freitag 2019; Lépine, Treibich, & d'Exelle, 2020; Cullen, 2022). The size of the response bias is usually around 10 percentage points. Misreporting often appears to vary according to respondent characteristics, education standing out as the most common heterogeneity dimension. Under-reporting of IPV is usually higher among educated women (Joseph et al., 2017; Agüero and Frisancho, 2022; Cullen, 2022).[20]

Few studies have so far explored misreporting in the justification of IPV and in the attitudes toward GBV with experimental surveys. Surveying adolescent girls in Bangladesh, Asadullah et al. (2021) find that support for IPV and for child marriage is considerably underreported when directly asked. Support for IPV is also underreported by men in rural central Ethiopia (Gibson et al., 2022) and by men in Bamako (Bertelli et al., 2025). Recent studies also document considerable response bias toward FGM, a form of GBV still present in Sub-Saharan Africa. De Cao and Lutz (2018) and Gibson et al. (2018) show that support for FGM is underreported by men and women in Ethiopia, where FGM is banned. In contrast, in Mali, where FGM is not illegal, Bertelli et al. (2025) show that support for FGM is overreported. This study also shows that in Mali, where the minimum legal age for girls to marry is 16, men do not underreport

---

[20] Joseph et al. (2017) also observe that the youngest and oldest respondents underreport domestic violence more than those of the middle-age cohort among a sample of women in the Indian state of Kerala.

their support for child marriage (that is, under 18 years old), contrary to the findings of Asadullah et al. (2021) where the practice is illegal.

5.2 Historical Determinants of Gender-Based Violence

Ancient structures of economic production and living arrangements may have contributed to the persistence of discriminatory gender social norms, including the practice of IPV. Societies where women contributed less to household subsistence have developed more discriminatory gender norms (Alesina et al., 2013). Historical cultural traditions relating to marriage – such as marriage transfers, patrilocality, polygamy, and endogamy – may also influence the practice and acceptance of IPV. For instance, patrilocality may make it more difficult for women to return to their natal families, leaving them more vulnerable to IPV. Similarly, in endogamous societies – where marriage occurs within a specific social or ethnic group – outside options may be more limited. On the contrary, husbands from nonendogamous societies would avoid beating a wife of a different ethnic group due to the risk of retaliation and conflict. While it is known that dowry is associated with feminicide (Bhalotra, Chakravarty, & Gulesci, 2020), the effect is more ambiguous for brideprice. It may increase the value placed on women's labor – decreasing IPV – but it may also make it harder for women to leave their husbands – possibly increasing IPV.

The work by Alesina, Brioschi, and La Ferrara (2021) explores these hypotheses. By relying on the Demographic and Health Surveys collected across 21 Sub-Saharan African countries between 2004 and 2016, matched with information about respondents' ethnic groups from the *Ethnographic Atlas*, the authors unveil that 28% of women have experienced IPV and that 47% of women – against 29% of men – justify IPV. Overall, there are more women who justify IPV than men in more than 80% of the ethnic groups analyzed by the authors. The study also documents that justification of IPV – by either women or men – is strongly associated with the historical use of the plough in agricultural production. Cultural traditions about marriage seem also to matter for IPV. Victimization is higher in endogamous, patrilocal, and polygamous societies. Men and women's justification of IPV is higher in endogamous and patrilocal societies, but somehow surprisingly lower in polygamous ethnic groups. Finally, the authors do not find any significant association between either victimization or acceptance of IPV and brideprice.

Two recent studies also explore the historical determinants of another form of violence against women, FGM. Corno, La Ferrara, and Voena (2021) test the hypothesis according to which the practice of FGM in Africa may be linked to the Red Sea slave trade, where infibulation was used to ensure the chastity of women sold as concubines. Their findings show that women belonging to ethnic groups historically exposed to the Red Sea slave trade are significantly more likely to have undergone infibulation. Specifically, a twofold increase in slave trade volume is associated with a 5.5 percentage point increase in infibulation rates. Becker (2022) examines another possible determinant, the practice of pastoralism. In pastoral societies, where men are frequently absent, controlling female sexuality may be a strategy to ensure paternity certainty. The author finds that a one standard deviation increase in historical pastoralism correlates with a 6.7 percentage point increase in the likelihood of infibulation. Both studies focus exclusively on infibulation, the most severe form of FGM. However, less invasive forms remain understudied. Some scholars argue that these less severe forms may stem from initiation rites linked to circumcision in both sexes, as observed in the Kono society of Sierra Leone, where excision is practiced without emphasizing female chastity or virginity (Ahmadu, 2000).

5.3 Theoretical Framework for Intimate Partner Violence

Economists put forward two main theories: expressive violence and instrumental violence. Expressive violence suggests that violence directly enters a man's utility or improves his well-being. The man may compensate his wife for his violent behavior with monetary transfers. Instrumental violence, on the other hand, posits that violence is used to extract monetary transfers from the wife or her family, to control the wife's behavior, or to manage resource allocations within the household.

The standard economic literature tends to explain the presence and persistence of IPV with household bargaining models, which examine how decisions are made in households where the preferences of two individuals differ. Noncooperative bargaining models are one approach, allowing the possibility of nonbinding agreements. The main intuition behind these models is that the perpetrator of violence weights the benefits and the costs of violence. The benefits may include expressive violence, which directly enters the utility of the perpetrator, instrumental purposes, stress (where violence is impulsive or used to release frustration), and status (where violence is used to restore men's status in the household). The costs include the wife's reduced productivity (as violence affects the victim's productivity), possible distaste for violence (as not all men derive satisfaction from perpetrating violence), and the level of the threat point – that is, the point at which the utility of quitting the household encompasses the utility of marriage. Household bargaining models represent the victim's bargaining power through her threat point (also called "reservation utility"), which represents the utility the victim would attain outside the relationship. If the utility within the marriage falls below her reservation utility, then the marriage is likely to dissolve. A higher threat point increases the victim's bargaining power within the relationship because the threat of leaving is more credible. As opportunities outside the relationship improve (such as working outside the home), the probability of leaving increases, leading to an intra-household distribution of resources more in line with the victim's preferences, resulting, ultimately, in a decrease in violence.

A set of theories specifically considers the link between economic resources and IPV. The standard *resource theory* suggests that women with limited resources are at a higher risk of abuse, while men with fewer resources are more likely to be abusive. More recent research, including household bargaining theories, focuses on *relative* resources, whereby an imbalance in spouses' resources may lead to violence. On one hand, women with fewer resources relative to their partner may be vulnerable to abuse due to marital dependency. On the other hand, women with more resources than their partner could suffer from violence too, as the resource imbalance creates stress from male status inconsistencies. A refinement of this theory, the *gendered resource theory* (Atkinson, Greenstein, & Lang, 2005), argues that the impact of relative resources on abuse is influenced by husbands' gender ideologies, whereby only husbands with traditional gender views perpetrate violence in response to a larger income share for women. In a slightly modified version to make it testable with the Demographic and Health Surveys data, Cools and Kotsadam (2017) propose the "contextual acceptance employment hypothesis" according to which women are at a higher risk of IPV if they hold a job in settings in which wife-beating is deemed acceptable by men.

5.4 Economic Resources and Intimate Partner Violence

Household bargaining models suggest that improved economic opportunities for women, such as higher wages or better employment prospects, can reduce IPV by balancing the power dynamics between partners. While it is generally assumed that women's employment should decrease the incidence of IPV, available data show a more nuanced picture. Crossing the information between IPV and FLFP across countries shows an U-shape relationship (Figure 12). In countries where women are mostly absent from the labor market, prevalence of IPV is above 10%. This rate decreases for countries with an FLFP between 45% and 60%. At higher levels of FLFP, however, IPV increases again above 10%. Some geographical patterns also emerge. Intimate partner violence remains low in Europe, Central Asia, East Asia, and Latin America, where FLFP is

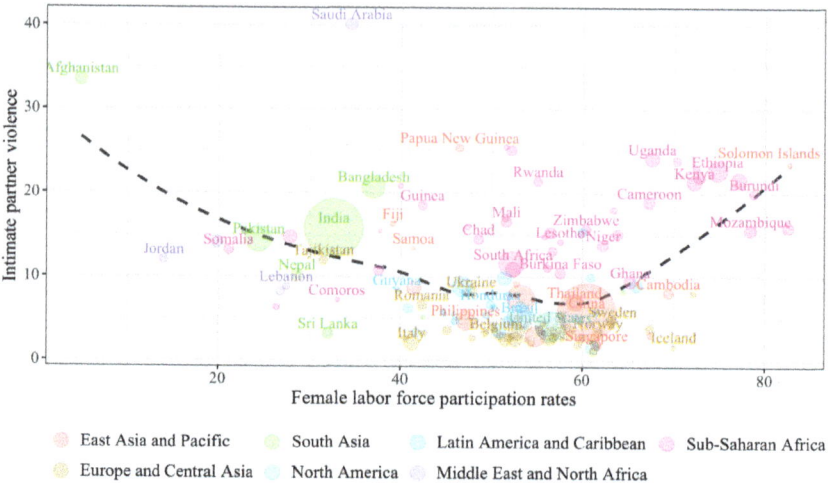

Figure 12 Intimate partner violence and female labor force participation.

Notes: Author's elaboration based on data from the OECD Gender Institution and Development database (2023) and from World Bank gender data (2023). The dashed line reports a nonparametric estimate of the cross-country relationship between the prevalence of IPV and the rate of FLFP. See Figure 10 for the measure of IPV. See Figure 5 for the measure of FLFP. Size of circles relates to country's population size.

between 40% and 60% (with the exception of Iceland, which records a FLFP rate of about 70%). In turn, in South Asia and the Middle East, where less than 40% of women have a work activity, IPV rates are higher. Sub-Saharan Africa and the Pacific Islands show a more dispersed trend, where IPV rates above 10% are associated with FLFP rates between 20% (Somalia) and 80% (Mozambique).

This nonlinear trend between IPV and FLFP is confirmed when looking separately at world macroregions. Regression estimates reported in Figure 13 confirm a negative relationship only for South Asia countries, whereas in Sub-Saharan Africa the relationship is positive. In the other macroregions the curve is close to horizontal, suggesting that IPV rates do not vary with FLFP. These different patterns suggest that women's economic resources may not always protect women from IPV, but that context-specific dynamics may matter, as suggested by Cools and Kotsadam (2017). The authors show, for instance, that IPV rates are higher in Sub-Saharan Africa for women living in areas with higher female education and labor force participation, especially if wife-beating is widely accepted.

Few studies – mostly impact evaluations of targeted policies – manage to isolate the effect of a change in economic resources or in women's access to the labor market on IPV. A review article by del Campo and Steinert (2022)

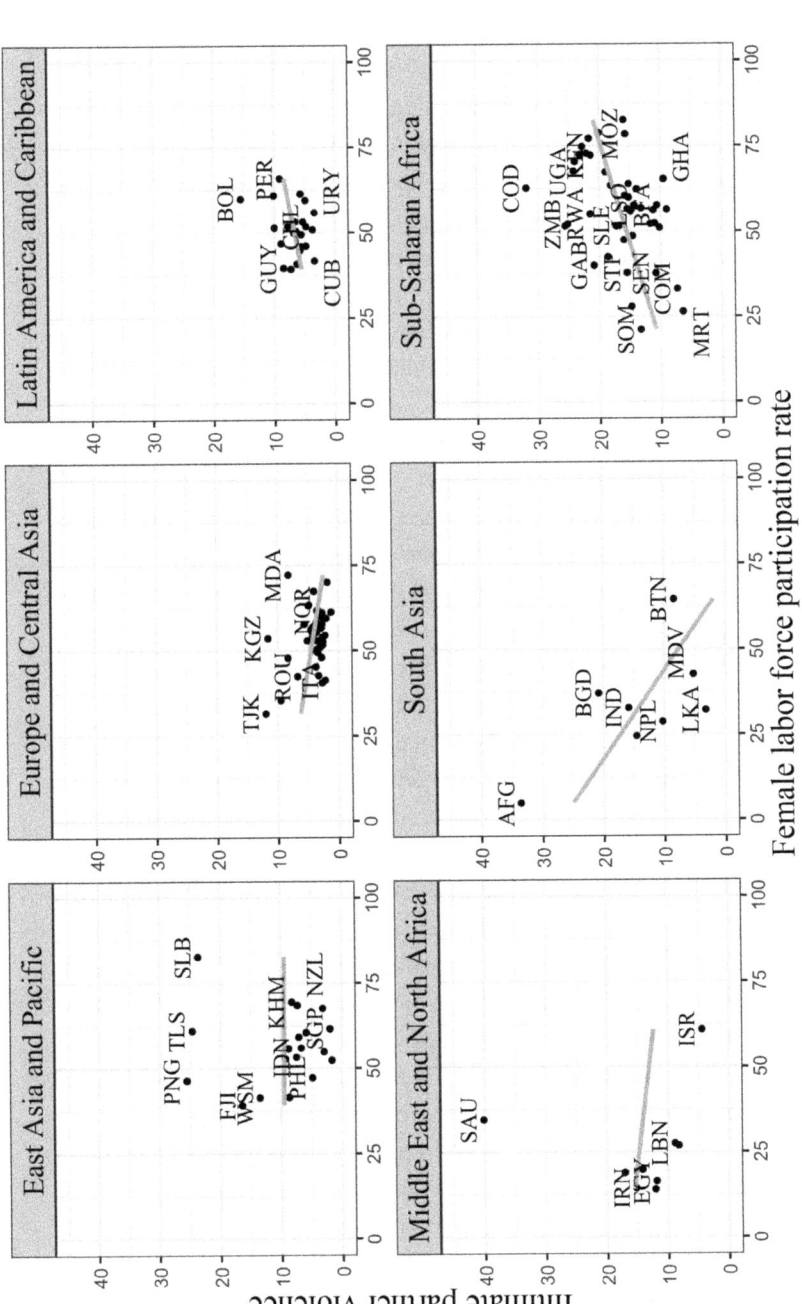

Figure 13 Intimate partner violence and female labor force participation by macroregion.
Notes: Author's elaboration. For the data sources and the definitions of the two indicators see Figure 12. The straight line represents a fitted linear regression.

provides a meta-analysis of 20 impact evaluations of the effects of economic empowerment interventions on IPV, spanning from 2006 to 2020 and observing the results between 6 and 60 months after the start of the intervention.

The meta-analysis results show a consistent negative impact, whereby economic empowerment results in a significant decrease in any type of violence – especially physical and emotional violence – across all included studies. The effect on sexual violence is negative as well, though not significantly different from zero, as few studies look at impacts on sexual violence. A subset of five studies includes a gender sensitivity intervention. The magnitude of all effect sizes is larger compared to effect sizes for the stand-alone economic empowerment interventions, though significant only for sexual violence. While the larger effect size may suggest that the additional gender training reinforces the violence-mitigating impact of the economic interventions, this remains conjecture due to the lack of statistical significance.

Importantly, del Campo and Steinert (2022) highlight substantial heterogeneity across studies. Four studies find an *increase* in IPV, mostly in the form of husbands' controlling behavior, in line with men using violence to extract monetary resources and/or to maintain dominant power. The authors equally stress using survey techniques to limit social desirability bias, as underreporting of IPV may be more prevalent in the treatment group, warning about the true treatment effect possibly being masked in studies relying exclusively on standard direct questions. This risk is indeed confirmed by a study by Bulte and Lensink (2019), who find that a training program targeting poor rural women in Vietnam resulted in an *increase* in IPV when measured with an LE, but in a decrease in IPV when measured with standard direct questions.

Closely related, an article by Baranov et al. (2021) reviews 14 studies evaluating the impacts of cash transfers on IPV. The meta-analysis shows a significant (albeit small) decrease of physical/sexual violence by 4 percentage points, emotional violence by 2 percentage points and controlling behaviors by 4 percentage points. Reassuringly, no study finds any significant increase in IPV. Half find a significant decrease, while the other half find no significant impact – though almost all report a negative point estimate.

Nevertheless, a number of studies find opposite results across subgroups, whereby violence decreased for some beneficiaries but increased for others. In particular, beneficiaries of the Mexican Oportunidades program are less likely to be victims of physical abuse, but more likely to suffer from emotional abuse and threats of physical abuse. Moreover, violence increased by 30% in households with husbands consuming alcohol and having no or little education. In Ecuador, female beneficiaries of a cash transfer program with less than primary education married to men with less education were more likely to suffer from emotional violence by 9 percentage points. Finally, domestic violence appears to decrease in polygamous households in Mali – where the husband was the cash transfer recipient – but not in Ghana, where violence decreased only in monogamous households and where the woman was the recipient.

Attaching a conditionality to the cash transfer may matter for decreasing IPV, as the need to fulfill the conditionality requirement might represent an additional cost of violence. Baranov et al. (2021) find that six out of eight CCTs decrease it, against one out of six unconditional cash transfers. A possible explanation is that men find the increase in women's economic resources less threatening if this is linked to children's benefits. In turn, the evidence is too thin to conclude whether other factors such as the recipient gender, frequency of payments, and payment size matter or not for IPV.

An open question is whether the documented effects on IPV are long-lasting. A work by Guarnieri and Rainer (2021) is one of the few relying on a historical natural experiment providing a long-term perspective. The authors explore the long-term consequences of the British and the French colonial systems in Cameroon on today's women's IPV and FLFP.[21]

Guarnieri and Rainer (2021) find robust evidence of a long-term positive effect of the British rule relative to the French rule on women's education and FLFP, resulting in wealthier households. Yet, they also show a significantly higher rate of IPV among women living in areas that were once under British rule. Women are about 10 percentage points more likely to have experienced physical violence in the past 12 months and they experienced about 0.3 violent acts more than those living in areas previously under French rule. The size of these effects is large, corresponding to a 40% increase relative to IPV prevalence in the region and to a 55.3% increase in the intensity of IPV. The authors

---

[21] The interest of looking at the British and the French colonial systems is that they differed along a variety of dimensions, including women's conditions. The former was based on indirect colonial ruling, allowing native chiefs into the local political system and granting equal rights to men and women. In turn, the latter system was based on French administrators directly ruling and implementing a policy of assimilation. Under the French system, women were excluded from the privileged status of *citoyen*, were granted fewer rights, and had restricted opportunities for formal employment and education. The education system was also considerably different under the two colonial systems. In the British system, girls and boys were taught together in the same classes, encouraging a high participation of girls. Under the French system, girls were excluded from the private schools led by Catholic missions and from the few public schools aimed at a small elite of native young men. Finally, women had different employment opportunities under the two colonial rules. The British abolished the German practice of forced labor, introduced cash wages, and developed tea cultivation (as they previously did in India and Sri Lanka) that was mostly done by women. In turn, the French kept the practice of forced labor and women were almost completely absent from the labor market.

show that these effects on IPV are explained by an increase in women's joint probability of being victimized and employed.

Among the different possible mechanisms behind the larger IPV rates found in past British Cameroon, the authors provide evidence in favor of a men's backlash effect, whereby men have a distaste for women's active participation in the labor force. Other possible channels, such as extractive violence or specific partner's characteristics, are dismissed.

This study points toward an interesting finding, partly confirmed by some of the studies presented here, whereby women's economic empowerment and participation in the labor market do not necessarily come with empowerment in the family sphere. Arguably, the British colonial regime did not provide stronger legal protection against domestic violence, despite facilitating equal access to education and providing an accrued access to the labor market for women. Still today, divorce does not appear a realistic outside option in Cameroon, where exposure to IPV does not represent a legal ground for divorce and where marital property is not divided equally between the spouses upon divorce. The prevalence of divorced women is almost null and only about 5% of women do not live with their partner. According to the SIGI, Cameroon today ranks among the countries with the highest level of discrimination against women in social institutions. As a consequence, granting women with direct legal protection against domestic violence and the ability to divorce, coupled with promoting societal and attitudinal changes, appears as a pressing policy issue.

6 The Overarching Role of Gendered Cultural Traits and Social Norms

Cultural traits and social norms favoring men over women, such as patriarchy, patrilocality, patrilineality, marriage transfers, and concepts of women's "purity" are among the cultural factors that might transmit and reinforce gender inequality across generations (Jayachandran, 2021). Likewise, mounting evidence points to deeply rooted discriminatory social norms as one of the leading causes for failing progressive policy reforms (see evidence discussed in Sections 3.1, 4.2, and 5.4). While feminist activists and theoreticians have for long urged to account for and act on gender social norms, the topic is the object of a more recent debate among economists. In this respect, a new literature, stressing the role of gender-related social norms for preference and habits formation, has recently seen an increased interest.

The definition of social norms is far from unique. They are broadly understood as a set of shared beliefs or informal rules about what is right and wrong, acceptable or "normal" within a social group. They differ across societies and communities because they are rooted in a specific cultural context. Sociologists, anthropologists, and political scientists have traditionally seen them as inherent to the systems and structures of society, permeating every aspect of it, being produced and reproduced through social interactions dictated by power relations between individuals and social groups. Social psychologists and, more recently, economists tend to focus more on the "individual" level of social norms. These are seen as collective constructs that influence an individual's beliefs about how to behave and about what others approve of or that affect the incentives and constraints of rational agents (Cookson et al., 2023).

The social psychologist approach to social norms has gained momentum in the development sphere especially thanks to the work of Cristina Bicchieri. Following Bicchieri (2017), social norms can be defined as those rules of behavior that individuals prefer to conform to on the condition that they believe: (a) most people in their reference group follow it (*empirical expectation*), (b) people in their reference group think they should obey it (*normative expectation*). In this perspective, social norms express social approval or disapproval of a given behavior and tell individuals how they ought to act. They are always (socially) conditional, in the sense that our preference for obeying them depends upon our expectations of collective compliance. Most people follow them because they know that they are generally followed and because they expect most individuals in their reference network to keep following them. The normative expectation influences the observed behavior.

With this approach in mind, several dimensions of gender inequality can be analyzed under the social norms lens. The very idea of gender roles is to define what is deemed appropriate for women and men, the attributes they should have and display in any situation. As such, gender roles are norms that women and men comply with all the time, affecting individual agency and replicating and reproducing the markers of what is considered the essential differences between the sexes (West & Zimmerman, 1987). Gender-based violence, including female genital cutting, child marriage, or women's unpaid domestic work, can be paradigmatic instances of gender social norms. Not only do people believe that those in their reference group will keep pursuing it (these are the empirical expectations), but they also believe that those in their reference group expect them to engage in it (these are the normative expectations). Consequently, they choose to align their behavior to the (perceived) norm, making the practice persist.[22]

---

[22] Based on the theoretical framework of Bicchieri (2017) it is hard to determine ex ante whether an observed behavior rests on social norms, as defined earlier in this Element. It may be a collective custom, moral, or religious rule, where conditional preference does not play any

The overview of the Gender Social Norms Index provided in Section 2 illustrates that gender-biased perceptions are widely shared across the world population. About 9 out of 10 men and women hold at least one biased attitude against women, the most common bias relating to women's physical integrity (justification of domestic violence and the opposition against abortion). As discussed, these views are strongly persistent over time and are shared by men and women alike. The widespread adherence to discriminatory behaviors or, put it differently, the identification of behaviors judged as appropriate along gender lines can be symptomatic of persistent gender social norms. In this sense, norms delimitating women's role in a given society are a plausible driver of the cross-country variation in gender inequality beyond the society's level of economic development. For instance, the presence of norms defining the acceptable job activities for women is part of the explanation for the U-shaped curve between FLFP and economic growth identified by Goldin (1994).

Several studies confirm the persistence of gender-related cultural traits transmitted across generations and across different contexts, influencing actual behaviors. Skewed sex ratios due to son preference are still present among communities of Chinese and Indian origin in Spain and in the United States of America (Abrevaya, 2009; González, 2018). In the United States, FLFP is lower among offspring of immigrants from countries that experienced the Neolithic revolution earlier on (Hansen et al., 2015), girls' likelihood to attend college is lower among descendants of migrants from countries with a "gendered language" (Galor, Özak, & Sarid, 2020), and fertility rates are higher among descendants of immigrants coming from countries with higher fertility rates (Fernández & Fogli, 2009; Gay, 2023a). The intergenerational transmission of different behaviors appears to occur mostly through mothers and mothers-in-law (Fernández & Fogli, 2009; Blau et al., 2013; Gay, 2023b).

6.1 Shifting Gendered Cultural Traits and Social Norms

Nevertheless, cultural traits do evolve, making social norms a dynamic concept. Under a policy perspective, the most interesting question is probably how to make gender-biased social norms more egalitarian to effectively change behaviors and to avoid backfiring progressive policy reforms. A recent blooming

---

role. Or it could be a descriptive norm where conditional preference is based only on empirical expectations without any normative component. Understanding whether a specific behavior makes the object of a social norm boils down to an empirical question that requires measuring empirical expectations, normative expectations, and conditional preferences, a challenging task most often absent from the economic literature.

economic literature investigates the type of interventions that successfully trigger changes in gender-related cultural traits and social norms.[23]

Historically, we know that some major societal events managed to drastically shift behaviors and (partly) beliefs. Massive historical shocks affecting the sex ratio, such as World Wars I and II, increased female labor force participation in France (Gay, 2023b) and in the United States (Fernández, Fogli, & Olivetti, 2004) with lasting effects over the subsequent generations of working women. Interestingly, Gay (2023b) shows that respondents born in French counties that experienced higher military death rates during World War I hold more progressive attitudes toward female labor, but not toward religion, marriage, or the family, suggesting that the shift in attitudes was limited to those specifically related to the role of women in the labor force. In a similar vein, the study by Teso (2019) documents that past sex ratio imbalances generated by the transatlantic slave trade in Sub-Saharan Africa still induce current generations of women to enter the labor force and to have fewer children and at a later age. The shift of gender social norms appears, however, somewhat limited. Women living in places heavily impacted by the slave trade are today more likely to participate in household decisions and to believe that men and women should be treated equally, but no improvement is observed in terms of attitudes toward domestic violence and beliefs about women in politics.

Beyond these major historical events, policymakers and scholars are increasingly paying attention at ways to effectively shift entrenched discriminatory social norms. The rest of this section reviews scientific evidence looking at the impacts of policy reforms, media campaigns, targeted interventions involving men, and correcting people's (mis)perception of mainstream social norms.

6.1.1 Legislation

As documented in Section 2, worldwide 40% of women and girls live in countries where laws and social institutions still exhibit a high or very high level of discrimination against women (OECD, 2023). These formal legal rules often mirror and perpetuate discriminatory social norms. Unequal inheritance laws, for example, entrench women's economic dependence by limiting their access to property and intergenerational wealth. Likewise, laws setting different minimum marriage ages for girls and boys not only reflect existing customs but also reinforce the idea that early marriage for girls is acceptable. Such legal disparities shape gendered attitudes, fostering the belief that women should remain

---

[23] It is important to mention that most of the economic literature proxies social norms with attitudes, beliefs, perceptions, or actual behaviors, making it sometimes hard to infer changes in terms of normative social norms.

financially reliant on a father or husband and play a lesser role in economic life. By embedding these inequalities into law, legal systems help sustain gender gaps in labor market participation and decision-making power.

In principle, introducing laws, with associated sanctions, against discriminatory practices could successfully curb those behaviors ruled by social norms. The sanctions would alter the cost and benefit of the targeted behavior, changing empirical and normative expectations. In theory, people are predicted to abide by the law if sanctions are sufficiently severe whereas they would tend to break the law if sanctions are too mild. However, to grant successful enforcement the law and the authorities should also be seen as legitimate and, probably even more importantly, the legal arrangements should not appear so distant from existing social norms as to lose credibility. The challenge for legal reforms aimed at changing social norms is that they should promote new behaviors while approximating popular views, otherwise the threat to seek enforcement will not be credible (Bicchieri & Mercier, 2014).

The weight of social norms is such that it can potentially hamper the effectiveness of legal reforms and targeted interventions. As illustrated at various occasions across this Element, the scientific evidence on the effectiveness of policy reforms in favor of gender equality and equity shows mixed results. For instance, as discussed in Section 3.1, legislation imposing equal inheritance rights for men and women has proven ineffective amid strong patrilineal social norms in the Indian context. Similarly, a comparative review of land rights reforms in Kenya, Rwanda, and Uganda documents that granting equal rights to land while promoting land titling and privatization is insufficient – and even detrimental – due to the prevailing patriarchal customary laws and patrilineal social norms that prevent women from owning any land (Djurfeldt, 2020). The implementation of gender equity policies may also suffer depending on the structures and dynamics of powerful groups, whether their interests align with those of the legal reforms or whether they can successfully act against them (Nazneen, Hickey, & Sifaki, 2019).

Legal reforms have also addressed GBV to punish perpetrators, in spite of a persistent and widespread justification of IPV (see Section 5). Worldwide, most countries have passed legislation against GBV, though with varying degrees of definitions and sanctions. As of 2023, out of 189 countries, only 25 report no legislation against GBV, mostly in the MENA region.

Recent evidence shows that laws against domestic violence can, in fact, change behaviors and social norms. Sanin (2024) studies the 2008 Rwandan domestic violence law and the 2010 Ugandan law, which was followed in 2015 by a Supreme Court decision that made it unconstitutional to refund the brideprice upon divorce. The Rwandan anti-GBV legislation is one of the most comprehensive and transformative ones that directly challenges strong patriarchal norms, not only by banning domestic violence, but also by outlawing nonconsensual marital sex defined as rape. Born out of the ashes of the 1994 conflict, the women's groups advocacy work was strongly backed up by key members of the parliament and government actors, which also granted effective implementation (Burnet, 2019). As the study by Sanin (2024) shows, in Rwandan genocide-intense areas – where male scarcity led women to marry more violent men – divorce rates went up and domestic violence decreased after the law enactment. Interestingly, the results point toward an intergenerational transmission of different gender norms. The younger generation living in genocide-intense areas exhibits higher bargaining power, a reduction in domestic violence, and its acceptance without a rise in divorce rates after the law enactment.

These results suggest that laws can act as catalysts for changing social norms and behaviors, but, likely, under certain circumstances. In particular, assuring wide societal and governmental support, whereby key powerful groups and elites back up the reform, seems key. As put forward by Acemoglu and Jackson (2017), the gradual tightening of laws is effective when in line with prevailing social norms. In turn, when laws are in conflict with norms, tighter laws can have counteracting effects, reducing behavior among law-abiding individuals but increasing it among lawbreakers. In line with this, Sanin (2024) shows that the anti-GBV legislation passed in Uganda was not effective, possibly because it suffered from a lack of support from key powerful groups, which might be symptomatic of the law being too much in conflict with mainstream social norms about domestic violence.[24] In contrast, changing the cost of marital dissolution appeared to be more effective at curbing domestic violence. After the Supreme Court decision reduced the cost of divorce by prohibiting the refund of the brideprice, and dissolution was already socially acceptable, women from ethnic groups where the brideprice was previously refundable were more likely to separate and experienced less domestic violence (Sanin, 2024). The importance for legislation to be effective to count on societal support and/or on support of powerful groups is confirmed by Gulesci, Leone, and Zafar (2024) who document the risk of laws backfiring. The study shows that Pakistan's new domestic violence laws increased women's self-reported IPV in ethnic groups with very conservative views on wife-beating and divorce. The authors argue that this illustrates the backlash effect of laws that are in stark conflict with prevailing social norms.

---

[24] According to Ahikire and Mwiine (2019) the final version of the law was probably too diluted to make any significant difference and suffered from a hazy implementation.

Another dimension of gender inequality on which an increasing number of countries has passed legislation are traditional harmful practices such as child marriage and FGM. The evidence here points toward a limited capacity of laws to curb these practices. In the case of child marriage, studies generally find limited or no impact of legal bans, probably due to weak law enforcement and persistent social norms (Batyra & Pesando, 2021; McGavock, 2021; Collin & Talbot, 2023; Wilson, 2022).[25] With respect to FGM, while some evidence suggests that legal bans can reduce FGM rates (Crisman et al., 2016; García-Hombrados & Salgado, 2023), other studies highlight significant limitations (Camilotti, 2015; Cetorelli et al., 2020; Kudo, 2023).

By comparing Mauritania, which banned FGM in 2005, with Mali, where no such law exists, Cetorelli et al. (2020) found no significant difference in the prevalence of FGM. In contrast, the introduction of an anti-FGM law in 1996 in Burkina Faso resulted in a significant decline in the prevalence of the practice, possibly thanks to the interplay between legislation and robust grassroots campaigns, which fostered societal disapproval of the practice and increased the perceived costs of compliance with traditional norms (Crisman et al., 2016). However, Kudo (2023) reports that the reduction was less pronounced for severe forms of the practice involving younger girls, underscoring the resilience of cultural practices that are perceived as important to community identity. The 1999 ban enacted in Senegal was found to effectively reduce the likelihood of undergoing FGM and simultaneously increased educational investments in girls, as parents reallocated resources in response to the heightened costs associated with FGM (García-Hombrados & Salgado, 2023). This contrasts with previous findings from Camilotti (2015), who documents that anti-FGM laws in Senegal prompted families to perform the practice earlier in a child's life to avoid detection, resulting in increased health risks due to the clandestine nature of the procedures.

It is somewhat hard to reconcile these divergent findings, as the effectiveness of a law is likely highly context-specific, depending on the country's political and social dynamics. A study by Poyker (2023) shows, indeed, that anti-FGM laws tend to be more effective in politically stable regimes, where people have greater trust in the consistency and durability of government enforcement. In contrast, in politically unstable settings, uncertainty about the enforcement of laws can weaken efforts to change deeply rooted social norms. This likely influences the capacity of legal bans to successfully change normative social norms by establishing a credible change in sanctions, in that the original negative

---

[25] See Section 4.2.1 for a discussion of the studies evaluating the impacts of bans against child marriage.

social sanction for not following the norm will be substituted by a new, credible negative sanction for following it. In this case, normative expectations would change, too (Bicchieri & Mercier, 2014).

6.1.2 Media and Edutainment

Beyond formal legislation, efforts to shift gender norms have included nationwide mass media campaigns or campaigns targeted at the community level. Exposure to information and different role models broadcast by the mass media has proven especially influential in shaping attitudes and behaviors. Despite not having this explicit goal, radio and television serial dramas that model gender-equitable attitudes, for example, portraying a father supporting his daughter's education, or a husband respecting his wife's decisions, have also been associated with shifts in audience attitudes and behaviors.

In Brazil, access to soap operas portraying small families led to lower fertility among women (Ferrara, Chong, & Duryea, 2012) and to increased divorce and separation rates (Chong & Ferrara, 2009). In India, access to cable TV is associated with improved gender attitudes (decrease of son preference and of domestic violence justification) and women's behavioral outcomes (increased autonomy, lower fertility) (Jensen & Oster, 2009). In Egypt, an anti-FGM campaign broadcast on radio between 1994 and 2003 reduced the likelihood of being cut by 13% among exposed cohorts under 15 years old at the time of the campaign (Khalifa, 2022). However, there is also evidence of backlash effects. Exposure to *telenovelas* with LGBTQ+ characters lowered tolerance toward homosexuals and homosexuality across 14 Latin American countries, the effect being larger among more conservative individuals (Gulesci, Lombardi, & Ramos, 2024).

Beyond exposure to mass media, the evidence about the capacity of targeted information campaigns or video messages to change gender-related behaviors and social norms is more mixed.[26] A recent review by Peterman (2025) looking at edutainment interventions on violence against women and children reports that most interventions are often found to effectively curb attitudes in support for violence, at least in the short term. However, their capacity to change behaviors is limited as most studies report null or small effects on violence against women.

---

[26] For recent reviews of the effects of edutainment interventions beyond gender social norms see La Ferrara (2016); Orozco-Olvera, Shen, and Cluver (2019); Grady, Iannantuoni, and Winters (2021).

In her review, Peterman (2025) reports that edutainment interventions against child marriage (eight studies) seem slightly more successful at curbing actual behaviors.[27] Among these, four measure impacts on child marriage rates and three find a significant decrease. A study by Raghunathan, Sushant, and Mankad (2021) finds a significant decrease in child marriage (−9 percentage points) and a delay in average age at marriage (+6.5 months) still five years after the end of the Breakthrough edutainment program - a large-scale intervention implemented in two Indian states combining a mass-media campaign urging men to act against child marriage, training about gender rights, sexuality, and sexual harassment targeted at key stakeholders at the community and Grand Panchayat level, and school-based training against early marriage. Interestingly, the delay in child marriage is coming from keeping girls longer in school (+9 months). Positive effects are also found in north Nigeria where a targeted edutainment intervention that successfully improved boys' and girls' primary school attendance and learning was also found to decrease the combined likelihood of teenage childbearing and marriage by 1.4–3.9 percentage points 12 months after the intervention (Orozco-Olvera & Rascon-Ramirez, 2023). These results combined echo those presented in Section 4.2.4 whereby several interventions find that increasing (girls') schooling manages to delay age at marriage. Moreover, these studies add an interesting piece of evidence: acting on the side of preferences with edutainment interventions is an additional successful way for promoting schooling and deterring child marriage.

Interesting insights about who shall be targeted within a community to transform gender social norms are provided by Cassidy et al. (2024). The study evaluates whether it is more successful to target an edutainment intervention – a mobile cinema screening of a street-theater performance against child marriage in two provinces of Pakistan – to men, women or both. Targeting men only significantly reduces the probability of female child marriage six months (−4.1 percentage point decrease, a 66% reduction relative to the control mean) and one year and a half after the end of the intervention (−5.3 percentage point decrease, a 43% reduction relative to the control mean). Targeting women only, who are considered more hesitant to depart from social norms about child marriage, is not effective, neither in the short nor in the long run. Targeting both women and men within the same household is effective only in the long run (−5.2 percentage points), but not in the short run. The authors reconcile these results with a theoretical model whereby women attach greater weight to the

---

[27] The review by Peterman (2025) also reviews four studies evaluating edutainment interventions against FGM, though only one looks at (and finds significant) impact on girls' cut rates.

sanctions of deviating from community norms than men do. Consequently, men would be more receptive of the intervention and would be more successful at persuading their untreated spouses to delay their daughters' marriage. However, they would be somewhat less successful in households where both are treated. To be convinced, mothers would first need to perceive the shift in community norms, making them accept to delay their daughters' marriage only in the long run. Women are found, notwithstanding, an important actor of change at the community level. Targeting women – either alone or jointly with their husbands – translates into similarly lower child marriage rates at the *village* level. According to the authors, mothers – given their stronger reluctance to deviate from social norms – would have greater incentives than fathers to diffuse information within the community to shift social norms, and they would do so through gendered networks.

These studies provide some new interesting insights about the mechanisms surrounding changes in social norms. Raghunathan et al. (2021) highlight that, despite a significant decrease in child marriage rates, the intervention did not make households hold more progressive norms about gender roles within the home. In fact, education is perceived as a vehicle for better management of the home rather than for empowering girls. Therefore, systematically interpreting changes in behaviors as changes in social norms can be misleading. Furthermore, behavioral changes at the household or at the community level may follow very distinct dynamics, especially when people strictly abide to community normative norms, as documented by Cassidy et al. (2024).

Several mechanisms seem to be at play. First, mass-media campaign and targeted edutainment interventions may improve people's knowledge, for instance, about the adverse consequences of violence, child marriage, or FGM.[28] However, behaviors dictated by normative social norms are hardly due to a lack of information, but most often to the fear of deviant behaviors being sanctioned by the reference group. Hence, the knowledge channel may, at best, affect individuals' preferences, but only change behaviors when these are not governed by normative social norms. Second, these interventions can also act on individual persuasion, whereby people are exposed to role models who behave in a different way or who directly tell them that their normative beliefs are mistaken.[29] This would be relevant for updating personal beliefs and changing behaviors dictated by descriptive norms, conventions, and habits.

---

[28] Out of the 21 studies reviewed by Peterman (2025), 11 explore impacts on knowledge and 9 find evidence of an information channel as potential mechanism.

[29] Peterman (2025) documents that out of the 18 studies exploring impacts on attitudes, 12 show evidence of an effect on individual persuasion.

However, it might not be enough to change normative social norms as people need to be convinced, in addition, that the large majority of their reference group is changing behavior and that deviating from the previous norm will not be sanctioned. Third, another possible channel is norms' perceptions – most often measured as changes in second-order beliefs, meaning people's beliefs about what the others think.[30] Yet the fact that a shift in perceptions does not translate into a behavioral change in most of these studies suggests that most interventions may have only affected, at best, empirical expectations, but not normative ones. For instance, learning about the illegality of child marriage might not change behaviors if the cost of deviating from the social norm is higher than the cost of deviating from the law, or if the law is perceived as not legitimate, too distant from existing norms or weakly enforced. Similarly, changing the perception of the community support for FGM will translate into a behavioral change only if people also start to believe that its abandonment will not be followed by negative sanctions.

In light of these mixed results, partly linked to the wide diversity of the study designs, and to the empirical challenging measurement of normative social norms, the literature on edutainment interventions has still much to explore. Future research would be particularly welcome for examining whether this type of interventions effectively changes not only attitudes and second-order beliefs but also normative expectations in order to trigger a change in social norms and associated behaviors. More studies are needed to test theories on how role models and storytelling influence attitudes, norms, and actual behaviors.

6.1.3 Targeting Boys and Men

Recent efforts have tried to shift gender-related behaviors and social norms by focusing on men. These interventions aim to address the role of men in violence perpetration, recognizing the key role that masculinity and gender-related social norms play in the acceptability and use of violence against women. Although not all men are violent, and some actively oppose violence, the use of violence over women is one source of power accorded to men in many settings. Mainstream masculinity indeed often entails dominance and control over women, which are attributes usually constituting the most legitimate and acclaimed version of hegemonic masculinity (Connell, 2013). Importantly, this dominant ideal of masculinity is not imposed but most often widely accepted as normal by both men and women from a young age. Most men aspire to it, even if they can't fully achieve it (for instance, due to poverty preventing a

---

[30] Peterman (2025) reports that, out of the 11 studies investigating this channel, 9 find a significant change in people's perception of what the reference group thinks.

man from being a provider), and it shapes shared views on how men and gender roles should be (Jewkes, Flood, & Lang, 2015). Thus both men and women need to be actively engaged to change this predominant masculinity ideal and gender-related norms.

A wide variety of interventions involving men and aimed at violence prevention are implemented worldwide; however, rigorous evaluations are scarce. A study by Ricardo, Eads, and Barker (2011) reviews 65 high-quality studies implemented in 11 countries, out of which 4 took place in middle-income countries (Brazil, India, Korea, and South Africa) and 3 took place in low-income countries (Ethiopia, Nicaragua, and Thailand).[31] Overall, only 8 interventions met criteria that placed them in the category of "strongest" quality, while 21 were classified as of "moderate" quality.[32] Out of these 29 studies, 15 evaluated the effects of interventions on perpetration of sexual, nonsexual, or both types of violence against women, as self-reported by men. The effects on self-reported perpetration of violence seems rather limited. Only 1 study found a significant decrease in sexual violence and 7 reported a decrease in any form of violence against women.[33] The reviewed interventions were more successful at shifting attitude towards violence (10 out of 16) and gender roles (5 out of 12), however for most studies there is a serious risk of these results being affected by social desirability bias as all outcomes were directly self-reported by men and little was done to address this risk of bias.

Recent evidence about engaging men alone in peer-facilitated group discussions aimed at transforming inequitable gender attitudes is provided by Vaillant et al. (2020) who evaluate the "Engaging Men through Accountable Practice" intervention with a clustered randomized control trial in North and South Kivu. The intervention consisted in a 16-week group-based discussion series for men with three-hour-long sessions led by male trainers. About six months after the end of the intervention, men were significantly less likely to intend to commit violence and to justify wife-beating, whereas they appeared

---

[31] Almost all studies (90%) took place in school settings and the vast majority (55) used group education methods to deliver the intervention. Only 27 targeted boys and men only.

[32] These categories were determined based on a Cochrane analysis. The following criteria applied to the strongest quality: individual or clustered randomized assignment with a large enough number of clusters, sufficient sample size (at least $n = 30$) at follow-up, follow-up of at least one month, no major methodological flaws or risks of bias. Studies fell into the "moderate" category if they had at least one significant risk of bias or methodological challenge, such as having a very small sample size, having sampling challenges, or problems with attrition that make results questionable.

[33] Of these, 4 were focused on early teens, 5 included both sexes in the intervention, and all involved prolonged interventions that addressed violence through promotion of respectful intimate relationships.

more likely to accept women refusing sex for any reason. However, no significant reduction in women's reports of physical or sexual IPV is found, even though women reported improvements in relationship quality and reductions in negative male behaviors.

Larger impacts were found by a closely related study investigating a randomized controlled trial intervention targeting couples in Rwanda (Doyle et al., 2018). Male participants were involved together with their female partners in a 15-session curriculum of 45 hours in total to discuss topics such as gender equality, fatherhood, reproductive health, and violence prevention.[34] The study found that, two years after the intervention, men in the treatment group were significantly more involved in caregiving and household tasks, showed greater support for shared decision-making, and were less likely to perpetrate physical or sexual IPV. Importantly, their female partners also reported improved relationship quality and reduced experiences of violence. These findings underscore the potential of structured, couples-based programs to shift harmful gender norms and promote healthier, more equitable relationships.

A different approach is the one evaluated by Nguyen and Tarp (2022), who tested two alternative types of interventions to encourage men to critically reflect about gender equality in Vietnam. The authors randomly assigned participants to two different tasks: either comment on national gender laws or write stories about gender equality. Those who wrote stories showed a 0.29 standard-deviation improvement in self-reported gender attitudes and a modest increase in housework contributions, while mere commentary had no effect. Simply pushing men to think about gender issues appears to change their perceptions of gender equality, even though it was not successful at changing their behavior, such as engaging in housework and providing childcare. Interestingly, this study also documents that providing information about gender-related laws does not change men's perceptions of gender issues, a possibly informative takeaway for those studies investigating the effectiveness of laws against GBV.

The capacity of a large-scale intervention to improve men's gender equitable attitudes and behavior is investigated by Alderman et al. (2025) with respect to Ethiopia's graduation program Strengthen PSNP Institutions and Resilience. On top of livelihoods and nutrition activities, the program had an explicit aim of promoting gender equity in two ways. First, men and women were brought together in village economic and social associations to facilitate discussions around financial literacy, savings and credit, income-generating activities, and gender equitable norms. The gender-related topics were discussed over six

---

[34] The curriculum was adapted from "Program P," an open source manual for engaging men in maternal and child health, created by Promundo, CulturaSalud, and REDMAS.

one-hour bimonthly sessions.[35] Second, men were invited to eight sessions of men-only group discussions to critically reflect on traditional gender roles and explore the positive and perceived negative effects of male involvement in tasks traditionally assigned to women.

Results show that at one-year follow-up men's gender equitable attitudes and their involvement in household tasks significantly increase. However, by three-year follow-up, only treatment arms with the men's groups continue to have significant impacts. Interestingly, the impact size is larger for men's engagement in household tasks (0.26–0.29 standard deviations) – such as cleaning, cooking, collecting firewood and water – than for gender equitable attitudes (0.07–0.14 standard deviations). Similar results are found from women's reports of their partner's behavior, mitigating worries of social desirability bias. This study underscores the transformative capacity of peer groups where men encourage and support each other to redefine traditional gender roles, effectively shifting attitudes and behaviors.

In this regard, a study by Pulerwitz et al. (2015) confirms the importance of group dynamics for triggering changes in attitudes. The authors investigate the Male Norms Initiative, a community-based intervention aimed at shifting gender norms and reducing IPV perpetration among men aged 15 to 24 in Addis Abeba, Ethiopia. Using a quasi-experimental design – caution should be used in interpreting these findings due to small sample size and lack of proper randomization design – the community intervention was either implemented alone or in combination with at set of eight group training sessions delivered in youth centers. The community intervention alone or combined with group training effectively decreases self-reported perpetration of IPV among participants. However, it successfully improved participants' support for gender-equitable norms only when combined with the group training. These results suggest that group discussion and education are an important component for interventions to effectively shift attitudes toward gender norms and masculinity.

While most studies focus on adult men, Dhar, Jain, and Jayachandran (2022) investigate adolescents' gender-related attitudes. The study evaluates an intervention conducted in the Indian state of Haryana that lasted much longer than those previously presented here. It engaged 7th to 10th graders in classroom discussions about gender equality, with a 45-minute session held every three

---

[35] The topics were the following: (1) workloads of men and women; (2) cooperation and sharing household work; (3) household decision-making; (4) improved listening, communication, and understanding skills; (5) engaging men in childcare; and (6) identifying restrictive social norms related to women's mobility.

weeks for two and one-half school years.[36] The program was found to significantly improve gender attitudes by +0.18 standard deviations in the short run (three and one-half months after the program ended) and by +0.16 standard deviations two years after the program ended. The program also appeared to improve self-reported gender-equal behavior, in both the short and medium run; however, more objective measures of behavior – whether girls submitted a college scholarship application and signing a public petition to end the dowry system – do not appear to improve. Interestingly, the study finds a significant and positive effect on attitudes and self-reported behaviors for both boys and girls in the short and medium run. However, boys report a larger and sustained impact on behaviors, whereas the effect on attitudes is less sustained for girls in the medium run. While the authors show that the results in the overall sample are not driven by experimenter demand effect, as measured by the Marlowe–Crowne social desirability scale, they do not show whether desirability bias matters differentially for boys and girls.

Even though the available scientific evidence is still probably too thin to clearly identify the key elements that make interventions targeting men and boys successful at changing gender social norms, a few patterns emerge. First, attitudes seem easier to change than actual behaviors, especially when it comes to perpetration of IPV. Part of the reason might be that changing attitudes does not equate with changing normative social norms (or their perception), making the last mile of a behavioral change hard to reach. Moreover, more evidence is needed to understand the type of men who effectively shift attitudes. Awareness might be more easily raised among those more sympathetic with gender equality and with the least propensity to ever be violent. In this respect, the selection of participants should provide enough variation among men to carefully avoid reinforcing gender-inequitable masculine ideals with the risk of further marginalizing men with different attitudes. Second, engaging the reference network, by reaching out to communities and not just individuals, seems to be more effective at addressing hegemonic gender norms than just focusing on individual-level attitude changes (Pulerwitz et al., 2015; Dhar et al., 2022; Alderman et al., 2025). This is coherent with the idea that norms are *shared* normative beliefs that require a collective process to be changed. Third, engaging both men and women, either in the same group-discussions (Doyle et al., 2018; Dhar et al., 2022) or by making women participate in related program activities (Alderman et al., 2025), appears to be an important aspect of successful

---

[36] The sessions taught facts and endorsed gender equality, prompting students to reflect on their own and society's views. Discussion topics included gender stereotypes, gender roles at home, girls' education, women's employment outside the home, and harassment.

interventions, as this possibly reinforces the message that surrounding social institutions care about gender inequality, updating the perceived social norms. Finally, one-size-fits-all interventions are rarely effective. Curricula must be tailored to local contexts and grounded in a sound theory of change. Evidence highlights the need to challenge dominant ideals of masculinity and gender roles, recognize similarities between men and women, and critically examine men's privilege and power to align it with women's rights and empowerment in the economic, political, and domestic spheres (Jewkes et al., 2015).

6.1.4 Correcting Misperceptions

People often tend to assume that others' behavior is consistent with their attitudes and preferences. By observing a widespread behavior in compliance with the social norm, people will infer that their reference group endorses the norm. When many people privately condemn a behavior but wrongly believe their peers endorse it, we are facing pluralistic ignorance (Bicchieri, 2017). In the absence of transparent communication among individuals, people may conceal their true opinions and align with the observed behavior to avoid being put at disadvantage. This may lead to the persistence of a behavior that most people dislike. Child marriage, FGM, and domestic violence can be the object of social norms subject to pluralistic ignorance.

Pluralistic ignorance occurs when people have wrong *normative* expectations (what they think their peers expect from them), whereas misperception of social norms occurs when people have wrong *empirical* expectations (how prevalent a certain behavior is). In the case of misperception, for instance, people may (wrongly) think that bribing is common in their country, and adapt their behavior based on this (false) empirical expectation. Whereas in the case of pluralistic ignorance, for instance, families decide not to cut their daughters without telling anyone because they think the norm is to cut the daughters and they would be ostracized otherwise. Both can be solved by either updating people's normative or empirical expectations, and this can help change behavior. Informing people about the actual frequency of a specific behavior can combat the original misperception of how frequent a behavior really is.

Misperceptions about others, being it in terms of their characteristics – such as race, income, tax evasion – or of their opinions – such as political ideology, gender equality, climate change – are widespread across the world. A review by Bursztyn and Yang (2022) shows that, out of 81 studies eliciting 434 beliefs, in only 20% of the beliefs the share of respondents who hold correct perceptions about others (i.e., within a 0.5 standard deviation of the truth) exceeds 50%. In more than 30% of the beliefs, more than three-quarters of the respondents hold beliefs that are at least a 0.5 standard deviation away from the truth.[37] Similarly, misperceptions of others' beliefs (second-order beliefs) are widely present across the world male and female population when it comes to supporting policies for gender equality in the labor market. Bursztyn et al. (2023) show that worldwide people underestimate others' support for basic rights policies, such as allowing women to work outside of the home, by an average of 20.6 percentage points. In 49 out of 60 countries this misperception concerns more than 70% of the population. The pattern is more mixed when it comes to beliefs about other's support for affirmative action policies, such as prioritizing women when hiring for leadership positions. This appears to be overall underestimated by 9 percentage points, though it is mostly underestimated in less gender-equal countries while it is overestimated in more gender-equal countries.

As mentioned, providing truthful information about others can be a strategy to correct misperceptions. The review by Bursztyn and Yang (2022) documents that, overall, updating people's beliefs proves to be effective in modifying their opinions; however, it is much less effective at modifying related behaviors, either actual or intended ones. Indeed, updating empirical expectation will be pertinent only if behaviors are governed by descriptive norms, but not by normative social norms (Bicchieri, 2017). Since a social norm is supported by normative expectations, it may be not sufficient to publicly disclose that most individuals dislike the norm and would like to behave differently. To change behavior, people must also be sure that its abandonment will not be followed by *negative sanctions*.

The literature on updating people's empirical expectation covers a variety of topics – from peers' voting participation to water and energy use, from savings to charitable donations (see the review by Haaland, Roth, & Wohlfart, 2023) – but very few studies have looked at correcting misperceptions about gender social norms. A study by Bursztyn, González, and Yanagizawa-Drott (2020) is a notable exception. Drawing from a sample of 1,500 young men (aged 18–35 years old) living in Saudi Arabia, the authors find that 82% of them are in favor of women working outside of the home, but 92% of them underestimate others' support. The study deploys an information experiment with a sample of 500 young men in Riyadh, whereby the true rate of support is revealed to one-half of the study participants. These are then asked to make an incentivized choice

---

[37] The "truth" benchmark is easier to determine for some objective characteristics – like the share of immigrants – whereas it is harder to assess when it comes to self-reported opinions, which, collected in standard surveys, may suffer from social desirability bias. Importantly, however, the study results do not appear to be driven by noise or measurement error.

between receiving an online gift card and signing their wives up for a job-matching mobile application. In the group receiving the updated information, sign-up for the job application increases by 9 percentage points (36% relative to the control group average). Importantly, the authors document long-lasting changes in opinions and actual behaviors.[38]

Overall, there is abundant scientific evidence showing that people widely misperceive others' beliefs and behaviors, holding concrete consequences for one's own behavior. Recent evidence also documents that perception of social norms plays an important role in gender equality, especially female employment outside of the home. Correcting those misperceptions is a low-hanging fruit for relatively inexpensive policies and it appears to be effective at changing beliefs and behaviors, at least related to women's work outside of the home. More evidence is needed to assess the effectiveness of this type of interventions in different contexts and for other gender social norms.

7 Conclusive Remarks, Paths for Future Research, and a Policy Road Map

The road to gender equality is still long, despite past progress. Improved access to reproductive health certainly led to a considerable drop in maternal mortality and adolescent birth rates. Wider access to family planning helped women take control of their fertility and family choices. Governmental efforts to make education accessible to all led to an increase in completion rates, for boys as for girls. Despite an encouraging upward trend in gender equality since the 1990s, the past few years have seen a stagnating – or even reversing – situation, especially with respect to women's access to the labor market. Besides, discriminatory laws and social norms persist, limiting equal rights and opportunities, especially in the global South.

This contrasted landscape lays the ground for a flourishing scientific literature in economics – and other sciences – that aims to understand the root causes of inequality and to provide sound evidence about effective solutions. Historical patriarchal norms related to lineage, asset control, inheritance, and the residency of married couples in favor of men play a key role in restricting women's human rights and preventing their human and economic empowerment. Economic growth and development may contribute to shift the dominant

---

[38] Three to five months later, wives of treated participants were significantly more likely to have applied for a job outside the home and to have interviewed for a job outside the home. The change in second-order beliefs is also persistent – whereby participants believe a significantly higher share of their neighbors in general support women working outside the home – and it appears to spill over to other behaviors – treated participants are significantly more likely to report that they would sign up their wives for driving lessons.

paradigm by, for instance, opening up new labor opportunities for women and making access to formal education less costly. Yet there is clearly room for policy interventions to facilitate and accelerate a much broader empowerment process.

The scientific evidence reviewed in this Element highlights that supporting female work activities and facilitating women's employment improve outcomes both at the woman level and at the household level. For instance, economic empowerment results in a significant decrease in any type of violence – especially physical and emotional violence. Similarly, cash transfers, particularly when attached to a child-related conditionality, effectively decrease domestic violence. Conditional in-kind or cash transfers, facilitating access to the labor market and providing school subsidies, also appear to be the most effective solution for delaying marriage and childbearing. Yet this is not to say that poverty and economic constraints should be seen as the only leverage for improving women's lives. While negative economic shocks can push households to adopt coping strategies detrimental for women – such as child marriage – policies providing simply unconditional cash transfers were less effective than conditional transfers and school-related interventions. Investing in girls' human capital is, in fact, a more effective policy response, showing long-lasting effects. Evidence shows long-term positive effects of keeping girls longer in school, whereby age at marriage increases together with their human capital, financial autonomy, and marriage mate quality. Interestingly, these results are not explained by a mere incarceration effect and, when contrasted with the limited impact of life-skills and vocational training found by the literature, they suggest that what matters is actual schooling and not just short-term training.

Another possible policy response for improving women's life conditions is to grant equal rights and opportunities to women and men. The economic literature in this respect is still thin and shows mixed results. Available evidence from the global South shows that legal bans against child marriage are partly effective, but mostly in urban areas. In turn, banning FGM has very little impact, as do reforms to grant equal inheritance rights. These discriminatory practices appear to be hard to curb, possibly due to a complex interplay between top-down legal reforms being too distant from the persistent social norms. In contrast, the expansion of formal pension systems – a policy not directly aimed at improving gender equality but acting on an important household constraint – was found to improve skewed sex ratios by making it unnecessary for parents to rely solely on sons for their old-age support. An important lesson to draw from these studies is that addressing the specific constraints or social norms related to certain practices may be more effective than banning the practice itself. Nevertheless, timing may matter too, whereby reforms may be effective only once the society is ready for change. The persistent and widespread approval for discriminatory practices still found in large part of the global South, and coupled with a limited state capacity for law enforcement, may prevent legal bans from being effective.

The limited available empirical evidence showing so far mixed effects of governmental laws and reforms lays the ground for more future research. The literature studying the effects of providing equal rights to women is richer in the global North and may provide guidance for future research. For instance, granting female suffrage was found to increase public spending in the United States and in Switzerland, especially the share of expenditures in public health (Doepke, Tertilt, & Voena, 2012). To date, evidence with respect to the impact of women's political rights on public spending in the global South is mixed and limited to the context of India (Chattopadhyay & Duflo, 2004; Ban & Rao, 2008; Clots-Figueras, 2011).[39] At least two additional topics could serve as the object of future research. First, the recent increase in the share of female parliament members observed among several developing countries may provide a fertile ground for more evidence in this respect. Second, more systematic evidence about policies granting legal access to contraceptives would be welcome amid the persistent high fertility rates and the unmet family planning needs observed in part of the global South, especially in Sub-Saharan Africa (Dupas et al., 2025). Evidence from the United States shows that granting legal access to oral contraceptives led to an increased control of women over the timing of childbearing, labor market participation, and bargaining in the household (Goldin & Katz, 2002). However, in poor countries the effect of granting legal access to the use of contraceptives may be limited by other family-level factors, such as women's bargaining power, questioning once more the role of cultural traits and social norms (Ashraf, Field, & Lee, 2014). In this respect, the economic literature assessing the effects of legal reforms on women's empowerment would probably benefit from embracing the "intersectionality" approach by accounting for the intersectional discrimination on the basis of gender, class, ethnic group, caste, and sexual orientation. This would possibly help to shed light on the complex dynamics behind women's empowerment in different contexts and across different oppressed groups.

---

[39] Following the Indian reform, pro-women laws regarding inheritance, violence, and crimes against women were passed (Priyanka, 2020; Clots-Figueras, 2011; Iyer et al., 2012) and an improvement in employment provision was observed, such as more NREGA-type public jobs that benefit women primarily (Bose & Das, 2018).

Future research is particularly needed to unveil the mechanisms and constraints on the household side that would make effective legal bans and targeted interventions for gender equality. Given the persistent institutional discrimination against women in low-income countries, more evidence is needed on understanding under which circumstances laws banning discriminatory practices and granting equal rights are effective. This requires analyses on a broad geographical scale, covering various countries, and on a broad temporal scale, covering multiple generations. Exploring changes in beliefs, perceptions, habits, and social norms would provide an important contribution to the extent that these factors can considerably limit the application and respect of any legal reform or targeted intervention. In this respect, shifting the vision of the discipline from a "women's affair" to include men's perceptions and behaviors appears to be a promising research avenue.

Besides, the measurement and methodological challenges faced by those studies assessing the evolution of social norms highlight the need for more data and of higher quality, especially when it comes to gender norms and GBV. As discussed in this Element, it is only recently that survey data about GBV started to be systematically collected at a national scale and concerns about lack of harmonization across countries remain. Moreover, data about victimization and gender norms are particularly sensitive to misreporting, making inference sometimes challenging. Increased efforts to improve data quality while protecting the respondents and granting their confidentiality should be taken as a serious concern by future research.

A broader policy-related question remains about the reasons for the lack of progress toward gender equality observed worldwide since 2019. Whether this relates – and to what extent – to the long shadow of the Covid-19 pandemic is yet to be formally assessed and quantified. Among the gender-sensitive measures put in place in response to the Covid crisis, more than half concerned GBV, while little efforts were put to strengthen women's economic security and support unpaid care work (Women UN, 2023). Open questions remain about the efficacy of those policy responses on gender equality. More broadly, shedding light on the consequences of crises on women and gender inequality is of paramount importance for building resilience and for promoting adequate policies in response and in anticipation of future crises.

Concerns about the future progress toward gender equality objectives are particularly worrisome given the recent cuts in Official Development Aid (ODA) targeted to gender equality and the decision of the new US administration to ban all public funding for international nongovernmental organizations working on abortion access and information.[40] This has concrete consequences for girls' ability to continue their education, for ensuring access to sexual and reproductive services, and for women's economic vulnerability. Based on global trends, this could result in 4.2 million unintended pregnancies and 8,340 deaths from pregnancy and childbirth-related complications by 2025.[41]

Even more worrisome, this funding reduction is starker in those least-developed countries with the lowest gender equality, suggesting a misalignment between gender-focused needs and donor allocation strategies. This is especially unfortunate given the costs of addressing gender inequality in the least developed countries are the lowest per capita than anywhere else in the world.[42] Today, 40% of women of reproductive age live under restrictive abortion laws, resulting in thousands of deaths from unsafe abortion each year, 270 million women lack access to modern contraception, and nearly 4.4 million girls are at risk of FGM.[43]

Furthermore, these funding cuts come at a time of new restrictive abortion policies, public health crises, and the rise of anti-rights movements threatening the progress made so far toward gender equality.[44] Against this surge in conservatism, some promising and forward-looking initiatives are taking place. A feminist approach to international aid has recently gained momentum both at the state level and within the feminist movement. Some 15 countries joined the Feminist Foreign Policy Plus (FFP+) group, a coalition of countries and organizations that support and promote a foreign policy approach to diplomacy at the international level. By putting gender equality and women's rights at the center of international relations, they aim to dismantle systemic inequalities by integrating a feminist perspective into diplomacy, official development assistance, and peace and security.[45] In parallel, there is a growing movement toward feminist financing, including the establishment of dedicated funds for

---

[40] The United States of America has historically been the leading donor for sexual and reproductive health and rights (SRHR), providing more than $9 billion in 2022; that is 66% of the total ODA for SRHR (DSW, 2024).
[41] See www.guttmacher.org/2025/01/family-planning-impact-trump-foreign-assistance-freeze.
[42] https://unctad.org/sdg-costing/gender-equality.
[43] https://focus2030.org/Gender-inequality-around-the-world-in-2025-special-report.
[44] Between 2019 and 2023 an alarming rise in funding for anti-rights and anti-gender movements was observed across Europe, amounting to US$1.18 billion (Datta, 2025). Moreover, in 2020 some 36 conservative governments, including the United States, have adopted the Geneva Consensus Declaration on Promoting Women's Health and Strengthening the Family, which opposes abortion and promotes a conservative vision of the family and the rights of sexual minorities.
[45] See www.ffpcollaborative.org.

feminist organizations, which advocates for allocating more resources to feminist and women's rights organizations, ensuring that funding reaches grassroots initiatives effectively.

Scientific research has an important role to play in the fight for gender equality. By documenting the best practices and assessing the effectiveness of policy interventions, scientific evidence can help canalize efforts toward those actions showing the largest impact and the highest value for money. In recent years scientific evidence has made remarkable progress in providing causal evidence about the root causes and mechanisms behind gender inequality. A flourishing experimental literature has also identified and quantified targeted interventions effectively improving girls and women's living conditions. Yet much still needs to be explored. It is only recently that the economic literature has started to systematically questioning the role of social norms when assessing policy impacts on gender inequality. Societal changes encompassing gendered cultural traits, beliefs, and social norms still need to be assessed with broader long-term analyses to ascertain persistent improvements. In light of the tremendous heterogeneities among countries in the global South, the role played by policy design to accommodate different contexts is yet to be fully understood. There clearly remain many important unanswered questions and a need for richer data and further explorations.

The road to gender equality is paved with uncertainties, putting at stake the lives of millions of women and girls. In light of the current trajectory of declining ODA flows, without a concerted effort to increase and sustain funding, particularly for programs targeting the most marginalized women and girls, the global community risks falling short of its commitments to gender equality and inclusive development. More than ever, there is the need for a large and comprehensive scientific and political push, which includes increased diversified investment, improved data collection, and a commitment to feminist and women's rights principles to ensure that gender equality remains a central focus of development efforts.

References

Abrevaya, J. (2009). Are there missing girls in the United States? Evidence from birth data. *American Economic Journal: Applied Economics*, *1*(2), 1–34.

Acemoglu, D., & Jackson, M. O. (2017). Social norms and the enforcement of laws. *Journal of the European Economic Association*, *15*(2), 245–295.

Addati, L., Cattaneo, U., Esquivel, V., & Valarino, I. (2018). *Care work and care jobs for the future of decent work*. International Labour Organization.

Agüero, J. M., & Frisancho, V. (2022). Measuring violence against women with experimental methods. *Economic Development and Cultural Change*, *70*(4), 1565–1590.

Ahikire, J., & Mwiine, A. (2019). Contesting ideas, aligning incentives: The politics of Uganda's Domestic Violence Act (2010). In *Negotiating gender equity in the global South* (pp. 67–87). Routledge.

Ahmadu, F. (2000). Rites and wrongs: An insider/outsider reflects on power and excision. In B. Shell-Duncan & Y. Hernlund (eds.), *Female "circumcision" in Africa, culture controversy and change* (chap. 14). Lynne Reinner.

Alderman, H., Gilligan, D. O., Hidrobo, M., Leight, J., Mulford, M., & Tambet, H. (2025). Men can cook: Effectiveness of a men's engagement intervention to change attitudes and behaviors in rural Ethiopia. *World Development*, *185*, 106781.

Alesina, A., Brioschi, B., & La Ferrara, E. (2021). Violence against women: A cross-cultural analysis for Africa. *Economica*, *88*(349), 70–104.

Alesina, A., Giuliano, P., & Nunn, N. (2013). On the origins of gender roles: Women and the plough. *The Quarterly Journal of Economics*, *128*(2), 469–530.

Alesina, A., Giuliano, P., & Nunn, N. (2018, 01). Traditional agricultural practices and the sex ratio today. *PLoS One*, *13*(1), e0190510.

Alfonsi, L., Namubiru, M., & Spaziani, S. (2024). Gender gaps: Back and here to stay? Evidence from skilled Ugandan workers during Covid-19. *Review of Economics of the Household*, *22*(3), 999–1046.

Almond, D., Li, H., & Zhang, S. (2019). Land reform and sex selection in China. *Journal of Political Economy*, *127*(2), 560–585.

Amin, S., Saha, J., & Ahmed, J. (2018). Skills-building programs to reduce child marriage in Bangladesh: A randomized controlled trial. *Journal of Adolescent Health*, *63*(3), 293–300.

Anderson, S., & Ray, D. (2010). Missing women: Age and disease. *The Review of Economic Studies, 77*(4), 1262–1300.

Angrist, J., Bettinger, E., Bloom, E., King, E., & Kremer, M. (2002). Vouchers for private schooling in Colombia: Evidence from a randomized natural experiment. *American Economic Review, 92*(5), 1535–1558.

Angrist, J., Bettinger, E., & Kremer, M. (2006). Long-term educational consequences of secondary school vouchers: Evidence from administrative records in Colombia. *American Economic Review, 96*(3), 847–862.

Asadullah, M. N., De Cao, E., Khatoon, F. Z., & Siddique, Z. (2021). Measuring gender attitudes using list experiments. *Journal of Population Economics, 34*(2), 367–400.

Asadullah, M. N., & Wahhaj, Z. (2019). Early marriage, social networks and the transmission of norms. *Economica, 86*(344), 801–831.

Ashraf, N., Field, E., & Lee, J. (2014). Household bargaining and excess fertility: An experimental study in Zambia. *American Economic Review, 104*(7), 2210–2237.

Atkinson, M. P., Greenstein, T. N., & Lang, M. M. (2005). For women, breadwinning can be dangerous: Gendered resource theory and wife abuse. *Journal of Marriage and Family, 67*(5), 1137–1148.

Badgett, M. V. L., Carpenter, C. S., & Sansone, D. (2021, May). LGBTQ economics. *Journal of Economic Perspectives, 35*(2), 141–170.

Baird, S., McIntosh, C., & Özler, B. (2011). Cash or condition? Evidence from a cash transfer experiment. *The Quarterly Journal of Economics, 126*(4), 1709–1753.

Baird, S., McIntosh, C., & Özler, B. (2019). When the money runs out: Do cash transfers have sustained effects on human capital accumulation? *Journal of Development Economics, 140*, 169–185.

Balasubramanian, P., Ibanez, M., Khan, S., & Sahoo, S. (2024). Does women's economic empowerment promote human development in low-and middle-income countries? A meta-analysis. *World Development, 178*, 106588.

Ban, R., & Rao, V. (2008). Tokenism or agency? The impact of women's reservations on village democracies in South India. *Economic Development and Cultural Change, 56*(3), 501–530.

Bandiera, O., Buehren, N., Burgess, R., Goldstein, M., Gulesci, S., Rasul, I., & Sulaiman, M. (2020). Women's empowerment in action: Evidence from a randomized control trial in Africa. *American Economic Journal: Applied Economics, 12*(1), 210–259.

Bandiera, O., Buehren, N., Goldstein, M., Rasul, I., & Smurra, A. (2019). The economic lives of young women in the time of Ebola: Lessons from an empowerment program. *World Bank Policy Research Working Paper* (8760). https://papers.ssrn.com/sol3/papers.cfm?abstract_id=3344844.

Bandiera, O., Elsayed, A., Heil, A., & Smurra, A. (2022). Economic development and the organisation of labour: Evidence from the Jobs of the World Project. *Journal of the European Economic Association, 20*(6), 2226–2270.

Bandiera, O., & Natraj, A. (2013). Does gender inequality hinder development and economic growth? Evidence and policy implications. *The World Bank Research Observer, 28*(1), 2–21.

Baranov, V., Cameron, L., Contreras Suarez, D., & Thibout, C. (2021). Theoretical underpinnings and meta-analysis of the effects of cash transfers on intimate partner violence in low-and middle-income countries. *Journal of Development Studies, 57*(1), 1–25.

Batyra, E., & Pesando, L. M. (2021). Trends in child marriage and new evidence on the selective impact of changes in age-at-marriage laws on early marriage. *SSM-Population Health, 14*, 100811.

Becker, A. (2025). On the economic origins of concerns over women's chastity. *Review of Economic Studies, 92*(4), 2303–2329.

Berniell, I., Gasparini, L., Marchionni, M., & Viollaz, M. (2023). The role of children and work-from-home in gender labor market asymmetries: Evidence from the Covid-19 pandemic in Latin America. *Review of Economics of the Household, 21*(4), 1191–1214.

Bertelli, O., Calvo, T., Coulibaly, M., et al. (2024). Men's justification of intimate partner violence: Results from an experimental survey in Mali. *Revue d'économie du développement, 32*(3)25–32.

Bertelli, O., Calvo, T., Lavallée, E., Mercier, M., & Mesplé-Somps, S. (2025). What one thinks, what one says and what one does: Male justifications and practices of gender-based violence in Mali. *Journal of Development Economics, 176*, 103479.

Bhalotra, S., Brulé, R., & Roy, S. (2020). Women's inheritance rights reform and the preference for sons in India. *Journal of Development Economics, 146*, 102275.

Bhalotra, S., Chakravarty, A., & Gulesci, S. (2020). The price of gold: Dowry and death in India. *Journal of Development Economics, 143*, 102413.

Bhalotra, S., Chakravarty, A., Mookherjee, D., & Pino, F. J. (2019). Property rights and gender bias: Evidence from land reform in West Bengal. *American Economic Journal: Applied Economics, 11*(2), 205–237.

Bicchieri, C. (2017). *Norms in the wild: How to diagnose, measure, and change social norms.* Oxford University Press.

Bicchieri, C., & Mercier, H. (2014). Norms and beliefs: How change occurs. *Iyyun: The Jerusalem Philosophical Quarterly, 63*, 60–82.

Blau, F. D., Kahn, L. M., Liu, A. Y.-H., & Papps, K. L. (2013). The transmission of women's fertility, human capital, and work orientation across immigrant generations. *Journal of Population Economics, 26*(2), 405–435.

Bose, N., & Das, S. (2018). Political reservation for women and delivery of public works program. *Review of Development Economics, 22*(1), 203–219.

Boserup, E. (1970). *Woman's role in economic development.* George Allen and Unwin.

Boudet, A. M. M. (2013). *On norms and agency: Conversations about gender equality with women and men in 20 countries.* World Bank.

Boulhane, O., Boxho, C., Kanga, D., Koussoubé, E., & Rouanet, L. (2024). *Empowering adolescent girls through safe spaces and accompanying measures in Côte d'ivoire.* Policy Research Working Paper 10721, The World Bank. https://openknowledge.worldbank.org/server/api/core/bitstreams/5d5379a8-ddf6-499e-a567-1ba7ecc19fce/content.

Bridgman, B., Duernecker, G., & Herrendorf, B. (2018). Structural transformation, marketization, and household production around the world. *Journal of Development Economics, 133*, 102–126.

Buchmann, N., Field, E., Glennerster, R., Nazneen, S., & Wang, X. Y. (2023). A signal to end child marriage: Theory and experimental evidence from Bangladesh. *American Economic Review, 113*(10), 2645–2688.

Buehren, N., Chakravarty, S., Goldstein, M., Slavchevska, V., & Sulaiman, M. (2017). Adolescent girls' empowerment in conflict-affected settings: Experimental evidence from South Sudan. *Unpublished manuscript.*

Buehren, N., Goldstein, M., Gulesci, S., Sulaiman, M., & Yam, V. (2017). *Evaluation of an adolescent development program for girls in Tanzania.* The World Bank Policy Research Working Paper (7961). https://openknowledge.worldbank.org/server/api/core/bitstreams/810ea54b-52c2-56bc-aa46-1931e9bae3ca/content.

Bulte, E., & Lensink, R. (2019). Women's empowerment and domestic abuse: Experimental evidence from Vietnam. *European Economic Review, 115*, 172–191.

Burnet, J. E. (2019). Establishing a strong political commitment to gender equity: The politics of Rwanda's law on the prevention and punishment of gender-based violence (2008). In S. Nazneen, S, Hickey, and E. Sifaki, eds., *Negotiating gender equity in the global South* (pp. 88–107). Routledge.

Bursztyn, L., Cappelen, A. W., Tungodden, B., Voena, A., & Yanagizawa-Drott, D. H. (2023). *How are gender norms perceived?.* National Bureau of Economic Research. www.nber.org/papers/w31049.

Bursztyn, L., González, A. L., & Yanagizawa-Drott, D. (2020). Misperceived social norms: Women working outside the home in Saudi Arabia. *American economic review, 110*(10), 2997–3029.

Bursztyn, L., & Yang, D. Y. (2022). Misperceptions about others. *Annual Review of Economics*, *14*(1), 425–452.

Button, P., Carpenter, C. S., & Feir, D. (2025). Introduction to the special issue on LGBTQ economics. *Journal of Economics, Race, and Policy*, *8*, 1–4.

Camilotti, G. (2015). Interventions to stop female genital cutting and the evolution of the custom: Evidence on age at cutting in Senegal. *Journal of African Economies*, *25*(1), 133–158.

Carranza, E. (2014). Soil endowments, female labor force participation, and the demographic deficit of women in India. *American Economic Journal: Applied Economics*, *6*(4), 197–225.

Cassidy, R., Dam, A., Janssens, W., Kiani, U., & Morsink, K. (2024). *Targeting men, women or both to reduce child marriage*. Institute for Fiscal Studies. https://ifs.org.uk/publications/targeting-men-women-or-both-reduce-child-marriage.

Cetorelli, V., Wilson, B., Batyra, E., & Coast, E. (2020). Female genital mutilation/cutting in Mali and Mauritania: Understanding trends and evaluating policies. *Studies in Family Planning*, *51*(1), 51–69.

Chari, A., Heath, R., Maertens, A., & Fatima, F. (2017). The causal effect of maternal age at marriage on child wellbeing: Evidence from India. *Journal of Development Economics*, *127*, 42–55.

Chattopadhyay, R., & Duflo, E. (2004). Women as policy makers: Evidence from a randomized policy experiment in India. *Econometrica*, *72*(5), 1409–1443.

Chong, A., & Ferrara, E. L. (2009). Television and divorce: Evidence from Brazilian novelas. *Journal of the European Economic Association*, *7*(2–3), 458–468.

Clots-Figueras, I. (2011). Women in politics: Evidence from the Indian states. *Journal of Public Economics*, *95*(7–8), 664–690.

Collin, M., & Talbot, T. (2023). Are age-of-marriage laws enforced? Evidence from developing countries. *Journal of Development Economics*, *160*, 102950.

Connell, R. (2013). *Gender and power: Society, the person and sexual politics*. John Wiley & Sons.

Cookson, T. P., Fuentes, L., Kuss, M. K., et al. (2023). *Social norms, gender and development: A review of research and practice*. United Nations Women. www.unwomen.org/sites/default/files/2023-10/discussion-paper-social-norms-gender-and-development-a-review-of-research-and-practice-en.pdf.

Cools, S., & Kotsadam, A. (2017). Resources and intimate partner violence in Sub-Saharan Africa. *World Development*, *95*, 211–230.

Corno, L., Hildebrandt, N., & Voena, A. (2020). Age of marriage, weather shocks, and the direction of marriage payments. *Econometrica, 88*(3), 879–915.

Corno, L., La Ferrara, E., & Voena, A. (2021). *Female genital cutting and the slave trade*. Working paper. www.econstor.eu/handle/10419/322156.

Corno, L., & Voena, A. (2023). Child marriage as informal insurance: Empirical evidence and policy simulations. *Journal of Development Economics, 162*, 103047.

Crisman, B., Dykstra, S., Kenny, C., & O'Donnell, M. (2016). *The impact of legislation on the hazard of female genital mutilation/cutting: Regression discontinuity evidence from Burkina Faso*. Center for Global Development Working Paper, (432). www.cgdev.org/sites/default/files/impact-legislation-hazard-female-genital-mutilationcutting-regression-discontinuity.pdf.

Cullen, C. (2022). Method matters: The underreporting of intimate partner violence. *The World Bank Economic Review 37*(1), 49–73.

Dahl, G. B., & Moretti, E. (2008). The demand for sons. *The Review of Economic Studies, 75*(4), 1085–1120.

Dake, F., Natali, L., Angeles, G., et al. (2018). Cash transfers, early marriage, and fertility in Malawi and Zambia. *Studies in Family Planning, 49*(4), 295–317.

Datta, N. (2025). *The next wave: How religious extremism is regaining power*. European Parliamentary Forum for Sexual and Reproductive Rights. www.epfweb.org/node/1147.

De Cao, E., & Lutz, C. (2018). Sensitive survey questions: Measuring attitudes regarding female genital cutting through a list experiment. *Oxford Bulletin of Economics and Statistics, 80*(5), 871–892.

del Campo, I. E., & Steinert, J. I. (2022). The effect of female economic empowerment interventions on the risk of intimate partner violence: A systematic review and meta-analysis. *Trauma, Violence, & Abuse, 23*(3), 810–826.

Dhar, D., Jain, T., & Jayachandran, S. (2022). Reshaping adolescents' gender attitudes: Evidence from a school-based experiment in India. *American Economic Review, 112*(3), 899–927.

Dinkelman, T., & Ngai, L. R. (2022). Time use and gender in Africa in times of structural transformation. *Journal of Economic Perspectives, 36*(1), 57–80.

Djurfeldt, A. A. (2020). Gendered land rights, legal reform and social norms in the context of land fragmentation. A review of the literature for Kenya, Rwanda and Uganda. *Land Use Policy, 90*, 104305.

Doepke, M., Tertilt, M., & Voena, A. (2012). The economics and politics of women's rights. *Annual Review of Economics, 4*(1), 339–372.

Doyle, K., Levtov, R. G., Barker, G. et al. (2018). Gender-transformative Bandebereho couples' intervention to promote male engagement in reproductive and maternal health and violence prevention in Rwanda: Findings from a randomized controlled trial. *PLoS One*, *13*(4), e0192756.

DSW. (2024). *Donors delivering for SHRH* (Tech. Rep.). Deutsche Stiftung Weltbevölkerung. www.dsw.org/publication/donors-delivering-for-srhr-2024-report.

Duflo, E. (2012). Women empowerment and economic development. *Journal of Economic Literature*, *50*(4), 1051–1079.

Duflo, E., Dupas, P., & Kremer, M. (2015). Education, HIV, and early fertility: Experimental evidence from Kenya. *American Economic Review*, *105*(9), 2757–2797.

Dupas, P., Jayachandran, S., Lleras-Muney, A., & Rossi, P. (2025, August). The negligible effect of free contraception on fertility: Experimental evidence from Burkina Faso. *American Economic Review*, *115*(8), 2659–2688.

Ebenstein, A. (2021). The historical origins of son preference: Patrilocality and missing women. Available at SSRN 3829406. https://papers.ssrn.com/sol3/papers.cfm?abstract_id=3829406.

Ebenstein, A. (2022). Elderly coresidence and son preference: Can pension reforms solve the "missing women" problem? Available at SSRN 4210110. https://papers.ssrn.com/sol3/papers.cfm?abstract_id=3829866.

Ebenstein, A., & Leung, S. (2010). Son preference and access to social insurance: Evidence from China's rural pension program. *Population and Development Review*, *36*(1), 47–70.

Erulkar, A., Medhin, G., & Weissman, E. (2017). The impact and cost of child marriage prevention in three African settings. *Unpublished manuscript*.

Fernández, R., & Fogli, A. (2009). Culture: An empirical investigation of beliefs, work, and fertility. *American Economic Journal: Macroeconomics*, *1*(1), 146–177.

Fernández, R., Fogli, A., & Olivetti, C. (2004). Mothers and sons: Preference formation and female labor force dynamics. *The Quarterly Journal of Economics*, *119*(4), 1249–1299.

Ferrara, E. L., Chong, A., & Duryea, S. (2012). Soap operas and fertility: Evidence from Brazil. *American Economic Journal: Applied Economics*, *4*(4), 1–31.

Field, E., & Ambrus, A. (2008). Early marriage, age of menarche, and female schooling attainment in Bangladesh. *Journal of Political Economy*, *116*(5), 881–930.

Galor, O., Özak, Ö., & Sarid, A. (2020). Linguistic traits and human capital formation. *AEA papers and proceedings* (Vol. 110, pp. 309–313).

García-Hombrados, J., & Salgado, E. (2023). Legal bans, female genital cutting, and education: Evidence from Senegal. *The World Bank Economic Review, 37*(1), 74–92.

Gay, V. (2023a). Culture: An empirical investigation of beliefs, work, and fertility: A verification and reproduction of Fernández and Fogli (*American Economic Journal: Macroeconomics*, 2009). *Journal of Comments and Replications in Economics (JCRE), 2*(2023), 1–15.

Gay, V. (2023b). The intergenerational transmission of World War I on female labour. *The Economic Journal, 133*(654), 2303–2333.

Giacobino, H., Huillery, E., Michel, B., & Sage, M. (2024). Schoolgirls, not brides: Education as a shield against child marriage. *American Economic Journal: Applied Economics, 16*(4), 109–143.

Gibson, M. A., Gurmu, E., Cobo, B., Rueda, M. M., & Scott, I. M. (2018). Indirect questioning method reveals hidden support for female genital cutting in south central Ethiopia. *PloS one, 13*(5), e0193985.

Gibson, M. A., Gurmu, E., Cobo, B., Rueda, M. M., & Scott, I. M. (2022). Measuring hidden support for physical intimate partner violence: A list randomization experiment in south central Ethiopia. *Journal of Interpersonal Violence, 37*(7–8), NP4238–NP4257.

Goldin, C. (1994). *The u-shaped female labor force function in economic development and economic history.* NBER Working Paper Series. www.nber.org/papers/w4707.

Goldin, C. (2022). Understanding the economic impact of Covid-19 on women. *Brookings Papers on Economic Activity, 2022*(1), 65–139.

Goldin, C., & Katz, L. F. (2002). The power of the pill: Oral contraceptives and women's career and marriage decisions. *Journal of Political Economy, 110*(4), 730–770.

González, L. (2018). Sex selection and health at birth among Indian immigrants. *Economics Human Biology, 29*, 64–75.

Grady, C., Iannantuoni, A., & Winters, M. S. (2021). Influencing the means but not the ends: The role of entertainment-education interventions in development. *World Development, 138*, 105200.

Guarnieri, E., & Rainer, H. (2021). Colonialism and female empowerment: A two-sided legacy. *Journal of Development Economics, 151*, 102666.

Gulesci, S., Leone, M., & Zafar, S. (2024). *Domestic violence laws and social norms: Evidence from Pakistan.* Trinity College Dublin, Department of Economics. www.tcd.ie/Economics/TEP/2024/TEP0324.pdf.

Gulesci, S., Lombardi, M., & Ramos, A. (2024). Telenovelas and attitudes toward the LGBTQ+ community in Latin America. *Labour Economics, 87*, 102488.

Haaland, I., Roth, C., & Wohlfart, J. (2023). Designing information provision experiments. *Journal of Economic Literature, 61*(1), 3–40.

Hahn, Y., Islam, A., Nuzhat, K., Smyth, R., & Yang, H.-S. (2018). Education, marriage, and fertility: Long-term evidence from a female stipend program in Bangladesh. *Economic Development and Cultural Change, 66*(2), 383–415.

Hansen, C. W., Jensen, P. S., & Skovsgaard, C. V. (2015). Modern gender roles and agricultural history: The Neolithic inheritance. *Journal of Economic Growth, 20*, 365–404.

Heath, R., & Mobarak, A. M. (2015). Manufacturing growth and the lives of Bangladeshi women. *Journal of Development Economics, 115*, 1–15.

Heise, L. L., & Kotsadam, A. (2015). Cross-national and multilevel correlates of partner violence: An analysis of data from population-based surveys. *The Lancet Global Health, 3*(6), e332–e340.

Iyer, L., Mani, A., Mishra, P., & Topalova, P. (2012, 10). The power of political voice: Women's political representation and crime in India. *American Economic Journal: Applied Economics, 4*(4), 165–193.

Jayachandran, S. (2015). The roots of gender inequality in developing countries. *Annual Review of Economics, 7*(1), 63–88.

Jayachandran, S. (2021). Social norms as a barrier to women's employment in developing countries. *IMF Economic Review, 69*(3), 576–595.

Jensen, R. (2012). Do labor market opportunities affect young women's work and family decisions? Experimental evidence from India. *The Quarterly Journal of Economics, 127*(2), 753–792.

Jensen, R., & Oster, E. (2009). The power of TV: Cable television and women's status in India. *The Quarterly Journal of Economics, 124*(3), 1057–1094.

Jensen, R., & Thornton, R. (2003). Early female marriage in the developing world. *Gender & Development, 11*(2), 9–19.

Jewkes, R., Flood, M., & Lang, J. (2015). From work with men and boys to changes of social norms and reduction of inequities in gender relations: A conceptual shift in prevention of violence against women and girls. *The Lancet, 385*(9977), 1580–1589.

Joseph, G., Javaid, S. U., Andres, L. A., Chellaraj, G., Solotaroff, J. L., & Rajan, S. I. (2017). *Underreporting of gender-based violence in Kerala, India*. World Bank Policy Research Working Paper (8044). https://papers.ssrn.com/sol3/papers.cfm?abstract_id=2959094.

Kelsall, T., Schulz, N., Ferguson, W. D., Vom Hau, M., Hickey, S., & Levy, B. (2022). *Political settlements and development: Theory, evidence, implications*. Oxford University Press.

Khalifa, S. (2022). Female genital cutting and bride price. *Unpublished job market paper*.

Kudo, Y. (2023). Eradicating female genital cutting: Implications from political efforts in Burkina Faso. *Oxford Economic Papers, 75*(1), 183–205.

La Ferrara, E. (2016). Mass media and social change: Can we use television to fight poverty? *Journal of the European Economic Association, 14*(4), 791–827.

Lépine, A., Treibich, C., & d'Exelle, B. (2020). Nothing but the truth: Consistency and efficiency of the list experiment method for the measurement of sensitive health behaviours. *Social Science & Medicine, 266*, 113326.

Malhotra, A., & Elnakib, S. (2021). 20 years of the evidence base on what works to prevent child marriage: A systematic review. *Journal of Adolescent Health, 68*(5), 847–862.

Mammen, K., & Paxson, C. (2000). Women's work and economic development. *Journal of Economic Perspectives, 14*(4), 141–164.

McGavock, T. (2021). Here waits the bride? The effect of Ethiopia's child marriage law. *Journal of Development Economics, 149*, 102580.

Nanda, P., Das, P., Datta, N., Lamba, S., & Pradhan, E. (2016). Making change with cash? Impact of a conditional cash transfer program on girls' education and age of marriage in India. International Center for Research on Women.

Nazneen, S., Hickey, S., & Sifaki, E. (2019). *Negotiating gender equity in the global South: The politics of domestic violence policy*. Taylor & Francis.

Nguyen, C. V., & Tarp, F. (2022). Changing male perceptions of gender equality: Evidence from a randomised controlled trial study. *World Development, 158*, 106019.

OECD. (2023). *SIGI 2023 global report: Gender equality in times of crisis, Social Institutions and Gender Index*. OECD. www.oecd.org/en/publications/sigi-2023-global-report_4607b7c7-en.html.

OECD. (2024). *Development finance for gender equality 2024*. OECD. www.oecd.org/content/dam/oecd/en/publications/reports/2024/12/development-finance-for-gender-equality-2024_06c6f365/e340afbf-en.pdf.

Orozco-Olvera, V., & Rascon-Ramirez, E. (2023). *Improving enrollment and learning through videos and mobiles*. Policy Research Working Paper 10413. World Bank. https://papers.ssrn.com/sol3/papers.cfm?abstract_id=4221220.

Orozco-Olvera, V., Shen, F., & Cluver, L. (2019). The effectiveness of using entertainment education narratives to promote safer sexual behaviors of youth: A meta-analysis, 1985-2017. *PLoS One*, *14*(2), e0209969.

Peterman, A. (2025). Edutainment to prevent violence against women and children. *The World Bank Research Observer*, lkaf002.

Phillips, A. E., Gomez, G. B., Boily, M.- C., & Garnett, G. P. (2010). A systematic review and meta-analysis of quantitative interviewing tools to investigate self-reported HIV and STI associated behaviours in low-and middle-income countries. *International Journal of Epidemiology*, *39*(6), 1541–1555.

Plummer, M. L., Wight, D., Ross, D. A., et al. (2004). Asking semi-literate adolescents about sexual behaviour: the validity of assisted self-completion questionnaire (ASCQ) data in rural Tanzania. *Tropical Medicine & International Health*, *9*(6), 737–754.

Poyker, M. (2023, 09). Regime stability and the persistence of traditional practices. *The Review of Economics and Statistics*, *105*(5), 1175–1190.

Priyanka, S. (2020). Do female politicians matter for female labor market outcomes? Evidence from state legislative elections in India. *Labour Economics*, *64*, 101822.

Pulerwitz, J., Hughes, L., Mehta, M., Kidanu, A., Verani, F., & Tewolde, S. (2015). Changing gender norms and reducing intimate partner violence: Results from a quasi-experimental intervention study with young men in Ethiopia. *American Journal of Public Health*, *105*(1), 132–137.

Qian, N. (2008). Missing women and the price of tea in China: The effect of sex-specific earnings on sex imbalance. *The Quarterly Journal of Economics*, *123*(3), 1251–1285.

Raghunathan, N., Sushant, L., & Mankad, S. (2021). *Can media campaigns change attitudes and spark actions to reduce early child marriage? Impact evaluation of breakthrough's early marriage campaign in Jharkhand and Bihar States of India. Grantee final report*. International Initiative for Impact Evaluation (3ie). www.3ieimpact.org/sites/default/files/2021-03/GFR-PW2.02-3ie-BT-Endline-Report.pdf.

Ricardo, C., Eads, M., & Barker, G. (2011). *Engaging boys and young men in the prevention of sexual violence: A systematic and global review of evaluated interventions*. Sexual Violence Research Initiative. www.svri.org/sites/default/files/attachments/2016-03-21/menandboys.pdf.

Robinson, J. A., & Acemoglu, D. (2012). *Why nations fail: The origins of power, prosperity and poverty*. Profile London.

Roy, S. (2015). Empowering women? Inheritance rights, female education and dowry payments in India. *Journal of Development Economics*, *114*, 233–251.

Sanin, D. (2024). When do domestic violence laws work? The role of social norms (September 25). https://ssrn.com/abstract=4967673 or http://dx.doi.org/10.2139/ssrn.4967673.

Sen, A. (1992). Missing women. *BMJ: British Medical Journal, 304*(6827), 587–588.

Sinha, N., & Yoong, J. (2009). Long-term financial incentives and investment in daughters: Evidence from conditional cash transfers in North India. RAND Working Paper No. WR-667, February 27. https://ssrn.com/abstract=1354883 or http://dx.doi.org/10.2139/ssrn.1354883.

Teso, E. (2019). The long-term effect of demographic shocks on the evolution of gender roles: Evidence from the transatlantic slave trade. *Journal of the European Economic Association, 17*(2), 497–534.

The World Bank. (2012). *World Development Report: Gender Equality and Development*. World Bank Group. https://documents1.worldbank.org/curated/en/492221468136792185/pdf/646650WDR0201200Box364543B00PUBLIC0.pdf.

Traunmüller, R., Kijewski, S., & Freitag, M. (2019). The silent victims of sexual violence during war: Evidence from a list experiment in Sri Lanka. *Journal of Conflict Resolution, 63*(9), 2015–2042.

UNDP. (2023). Gender Social Norms Index (GSNI). UNDP (United Nations Development Programme). https://hdr.undp.org/system/files/documents/hdp-document/gsni202303.pdf.

United Nations Children's Fund. (2023). *Is an end to child marriage within reach? Latest trends and future prospects.* UNICEF. https://data.unicef.org/resources/is-an-end-to-child-marriage-within-reach.

Vaillant, J., Koussoubé, E., Roth, D., Pierotti, R., Hossain, M., & Falb, K. L. (2020). Engaging men to transform inequitable gender attitudes and prevent intimate partner violence: A cluster randomised controlled trial in North and South Kivu, Democratic Republic of Congo. *BMJ Global Health, 5*(5), 1–14.

WEF. (2022). *Global gender gap report*. World Economic Forum. www.weforum.org/publications/global-gender-gap-report-2022.

WEF. (2024). *Global gender gap report*. World Economic Forum. www.weforum.org/publications/global-gender-gap-report-2024.

West, C., & Zimmerman, D. H. (1987). Doing gender. *Gender & society, 1*(2), 125–151.

WHO. (2021). *Violence against women prevalence estimates, 2018: Global, regional and national prevalence estimates for intimate partner violence against women and global and regional prevalence estimates for non-partner sexual violence against women.* World Health Organization.

Wilson, N. (2022). Child marriage bans and female schooling and labor market outcomes: Evidence from natural experiments in 17 low-and middle-income countries. *American Economic Journal: Economic Policy*, *14*(3), 449–477.

Women UN. (2023). Promising practices for gender equality: A catalogue of practical solutions learned from the COVID-19 global response. *UNDP and UN Women*. www.unwomen.org/sites/default/files/2023-09/promising-practices-for-gender-equality-en.pdf.

Acknowledgments

I would like to thank UNU-WIDER, and especially Kunal Sen, the editor of the Elements Series in Development Economics, for offering me the opportunity to conduct extensive research on recent scientific studies exploring gender inequalities in the global South. I equally thank two anonymous referees for helpful comments and Pauline Aribaud for providing excellent research assistance. A special thank goes to all my students without whom this Element would not have been possible. I dedicate this Element to my daughter Gaïa, the most precious young woman of my life.

Cambridge Elements

Development Economics

Series Editor-in-Chief
Kunal Sen
UNU-WIDER and University of Manchester

Kunal Sen, UNU-WIDER Director, is Editor-in-Chief of the Cambridge Elements in Development Economics series. Professor Sen has over three decades of experience in academic and applied development economics research, and has carried out extensive work on international finance, the political economy of inclusive growth, the dynamics of poverty, social exclusion, female labour force participation, and the informal sector in developing economies. His research has focused on India, East Asia, and sub-Saharan Africa.

In addition to his work as Professor of Development Economics at the University of Manchester, Kunal has been the Joint Research Director of the Effective States and Inclusive Development (ESID) Research Centre, and a Research Fellow at the Institute for Labor Economics (IZA). He has also served in advisory roles with national governments and bilateral and multilateral development agencies, including the UK's Department for International Development, Asian Development Bank, and the International Development Research Centre.

Thematic Editors
Tony Addison
University of Copenhagen and UNU-WIDER

Tony Addison is a Professor of Economics in the University of Copenhagen's Development Economics Research Group. He is also a Non-Resident Senior Research Fellow at UNU-WIDER, Helsinki, where he was previously the Chief Economist-Deputy Director. In addition, he is Professor of Development Studies at the University of Manchester. His research interests focus on the extractive industries, energy transition, and macroeconomic policy for development.

Chris Barrett
SC Johnson College of Business, Cornell University

Chris Barrett is an agricultural and development economist at Cornell University. He is the Stephen B. and Janice G. Ashley Professor of Applied Economics and Management; and International Professor of Agriculture at the Charles H. Dyson School of Applied Economics and Management. He is also an elected Fellow of the American Association for the Advancement of Science, the Agricultural and Applied Economics Association, and the African Association of Agricultural Economists.

Carlos Gradín
University of Vigo

Carlos Gradín is a professor of applied economics at the University of Vigo. His main research interest is the study of inequalities, with special attention to those that exist between population groups (e.g., by race or sex). His publications have contributed to improving the empirical evidence in developing and developed countries, as well as globally, and to improving the available data and methods used.

Rachel M. Gisselquist
UNU-WIDER

Rachel M. Gisselquist is a Senior Research Fellow and member of the Senior Management Team of UNU-WIDER. She specializes in the comparative politics of developing countries, with particular attention to issues of inequality, ethnic and identity politics, foreign aid and state building, democracy and governance, and sub-Saharan African politics. Dr Gisselquist has edited a dozen collections in these areas, and her articles are published in a range of leading journals.

Shareen Joshi
Georgetown University

Shareen Joshi is an Associate Professor of International Development at Georgetown University's School of Foreign Service in the United States. Her research focuses on issues of inequality, human capital investment and grassroots collective action in South Asia. Her work has been published in the fields of development economics, population studies, environmental studies and gender studies.

Patricia Justino
UNU-WIDER and IDS – UK

Patricia Justino is a Senior Research Fellow at UNU-WIDER and Professorial Fellow at the Institute of Development Studies (IDS) (on leave). Her research focuses on the relationship between political violence, governance and development outcomes. She has published widely in the fields of development economics and political economy and is the co-founder and co-director of the Households in Conflict Network (HiCN).

Marinella Leone
University of Pavia

Marinella Leone is an assistant professor at the Department of Economics and Management, University of Pavia, Italy. She is an applied development economist. Her more recent research focuses on the study of early child development parenting programmes, on education, and gender-based violence. In previous research she investigated the short-, long-term and intergenerational impact of conflicts on health, education and domestic violence. She has published in top journals in economics and development economics.

Jukka Pirttilä
University of Helsinki and UNU-WIDER

Jukka Pirttilä is Professor of Public Economics at the University of Helsinki and VATT Institute for Economic Research. He is also a Non-Resident Senior Research Fellow at UNU-WIDER. His research focuses on tax policy, especially for developing countries. He is a co-principal investigator at the Finnish Centre of Excellence in Tax Systems Research.

Andy Sumner
King's College London and UNU-WIDER

Andy Sumner is Professor of International Development at King's College London; a Non-Resident Senior Fellow at UNU-WIDER and a Fellow of the Academy of Social Sciences. He has published extensively in the areas of poverty, inequality, and economic development.

About the Series

Cambridge Elements in Development Economics is led by UNU-WIDER in partnership with Cambridge University Press. The series publishes authoritative studies on important topics in the field covering both micro and macro aspects of development economics.

United Nations University World Institute for Development Economics Research

United Nations University World Institute for Development Economics Research (UNU-WIDER) provides economic analysis and policy advice aiming to promote sustainable and equitable development for all. The institute began operations in 1985 in Helsinki, Finland, as the first research centre of the United Nations University. Today, it is one of the world's leading development economics think tanks, working closely with a vast network of academic researchers and policy makers, mostly based in the Global South.

Cambridge Elements

Development Economics

Elements in the Series

Economic Transformation and Income Distribution in China over Three Decades
Cai Meng, Bjorn Gustafsson and John Knight

Chilean Economic Development under Neoliberalism: Structural Transformation, High Inequality and Environmental Fragility
Andrés Solimano and Gabriela Zapata-Román

Hierarchy of Needs and the Measurement of Poverty and Standards of Living
Joseph Deutsch and Jacques Silber

New Structural Financial Economics: A Framework for Rethinking the Role of Finance in Serving the Real Economy
Justin Yifu Lin, Jiajun Xu, Zirong Yang and Yilin Zhang

Knowledge and Global Inequality Since 1800: Interrogating the Present as History
Dev Nathan

Survival of the Greenest: Economic Transformation in a Climate-conscious World
Amir Lebdioui

Escaping Poverty Traps and Unlocking Prosperity in the Face of Climate Risk: Lessons from Index-Based Livestock Insurance
Nathaniel D. Jensen, Francesco P. Fava, Andrew G. Mude, Christopher B. Barrett, Brenda Wandera-Gache, Anton Vrieling, Masresha Taye, Kazushi Takahashi, Felix Lung, Munenobu Ikegami, Polly Ericksen, Philemon Chelanga, Sommarat Chantarat, Michael Carter, Hassan Bashir and Rupsha Banerjee

Financing for Development: The Global Agenda
José Antonio Ocampo

Poverty in Latin America: Feelings/Perceptions vs Material Conditions
Verónica Amarante, Maira Colacce and Federico Scalese

Trade in Tasks: A New Perspective to International Trade, Structural Change and Economic Development
Gaaitzen J. de Vries and Marcel P. Timmer

Developmental Dilemmas: The Role of Power and Agency
William D. Ferguson

Gender Economics in the Global South
Olivia Bertelli

A full series listing is available at: www.cambridge.org/CEDE

For EU product safety concerns, contact us at Calle de José Abascal, 56–1°,
28003 Madrid, Spain or eugpsr@cambridge.org.

www.ingramcontent.com/pod-product-compliance
Ingram Content Group UK Ltd.
Pitfield, Milton Keynes, MK11 3LW, UK
UKHW022113130426
469895UK00013B/179